T.I.S.S.U.E.S

A BOOK OF POETRY AND LIFE

D. SERVANT

WRITTEN BY DANIEL 'D. SERVANT' MENDES

Published by
Chipmunkapublishing
United Kingdom

http://www.chipmunkapublishing.com

Copyright © 2020 Daniel "D.Servant" Mendes

Believe

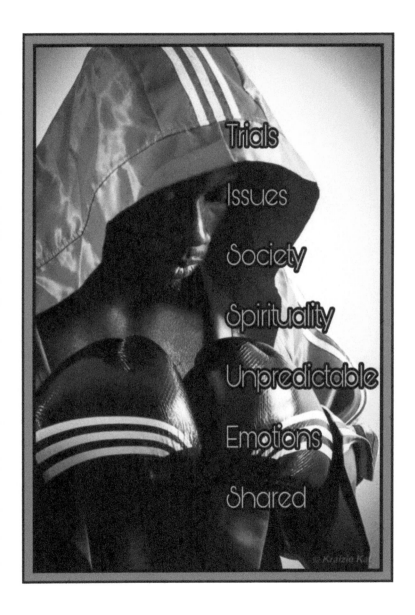

Trials

Issues

Society

Spirituality

Unpredictable

Emotions

Shared

Believe

Believe

Where a great struggle is,

there is also a strength greater

in that exact   same place'

Daniel 'D. Servant' Mendes

Believe

Believe

CONTENTS

THE OLD CHRONICLES (TOC)

Believe

Believe

.

THE NEW CHRONICLES (TNC)

Believe

Believe

Acknowledgements

Miss Forbes of Waverley School, Hob Moor Road, Small Heath Birmingham played a crucial role in my secondary school education, right up until my permanent exclusion. She was an English teacher of the highest pedigree.
Whilst studying Shakespeare's 'Romeo and Juliet' in the late 90's, the TV and VCR were wheeled into the classroom. Miss Forbes appeared baffled and was eventually driven to ask us students how to operate the electrical equipment.

One of my classmates, who was clearly humoured by the confusion, asked "What Miss, you don't know how to use it." She replied calmly, "No, I do not have one of these at home, I do not watch television."
The student continued, "So what do you do?" He was (like all of us) interested in how she spent her free time.
Miss Forbes countered passively, "I read books". I could not identify with that lifestyle but I equally could not mock it.

I have the utmost respect for Miss Forbes who laid the foundations of my English knowledge. I hope that she can be proud of her labour, especially due to its continued positive impact on my use of the English language. Miss Forbes together with my PE teacher, Mr Burgher have effortlessly earned my continued respect for their commitment to their subjects and their admirable self-conduct.

My family, the upbringing, the struggle that has stalked me throughout my journey of life, ironically inspired me to go from strength to strength. I pay special homage to the household that I grew up in which included myself, my mum and older brother, Anthony. I pay tribute to My Father, Step Father Ian Yearwood, Uncles and Aunties, Grandparents and my older cousins, who were notable influences growing up that I could observe and learn from in some way, but also who continue to collectively be examples of strong black males and females to this very day.

Believe

To all of my brothers and sisters, cousins, nieces, nephews, I love you all.

Sparkhill, Birmingham where I spent my childhood, B11 4JF where I possibly met my first friend ever, James Clarke. Small Heath, Birmingham where I spent most of my teenage years. Johara Choudhury. Stoke-on-Trent. Rob and Andy Fenton, Dionne Lewis. London. Travis Sweeney. Monique Jamera. Iss Brown, Arron Lennon (Lion Heart). Yves Bagouendi, Harry Zihni, Richard Edwards, Anthony Nicholls, Sharmen Begum, Christopher Emmanuel Longe, Bantu Masta, Abu Bakar, Omar 'Ali' Ahsan.

Leon Francis and Matthew Gayle RIP.

Musicians: Bjork, Tracy Chapman, Lauryn Hill, Queen Latifah, Erykah Badu, Sade, Alicia Keys, Madonna, Floetry, Mia X, Speech Debelle, Lady Leshurr, Aruba Red, Laura Mvula, Delilah, Rebecca Ferguson, Lisa Hannigan, The Chicks, Ghetto Twinz, Eternia, 3D Na'Tee, Jucee Froot, Solange Knowles.

Kano, Giggs, D Double E, Wiley, Devlin, President T, Ashley Walters, Skepta, JME, Cutch-I, Remtrex, Genny From The Block, Izzy Loc, Monster Vibrations, RM, RK, Devilman, Jaykae, Potter Payper, ASCO, Mist, Mike Skinner (The Streets), Ghetts, Nines, Fekky, Dizzee Rascal, SkinnyMan, Life MC, Ghostpoet, David Adonis, Michael Kiwanuka, Natty.

Ice-T (I Must Stand), Tupac Shakur, The Outlawz, Marvin Gaye, Seal, Mc Eiht, Spice1, Eazy-E, Bone Thugs N Harmony, The Lost Boyz, Paris, Rakim, Nas, Cormega, DMX, Jadakiss, Xzibit, Saigon, Papoose, Yasin Bey (Mos Def), Shyne, Shyheim, Talib Kweli, Juvenile, Blac Haze, The Jacka, Joe Blow, Husalah, Berner, AP.9, C-Murder, Master P, Silkk The Shocker, MAC, Mr Serv-On, Fiend, Big Pun, Big L, CNN, Andre Nickatina, Curren$y, Project Pat, Eminem, Young Buck, Kodak Black, Playa Fly, Peezy, Babyface Ray, Mobb Deep, Yukmouth, Waka Flocka Flame, Cozz, CEE Brown, K-Prez.

Believe

Bob Marley, Stephen Marley, Ziggy Marley, Burning Spear, Garnet Silk, Capleton, Sizzla, Lutan Fyah, Richie Spice, Turbulence, Promoe, Limp Bizkit, Linkin Park, Massive Attack, Vegyn.

Other inspirations: Harriet Tubman, Mother Teresa, Princess Diana, Shaka Zulu, Malcolm X, Marcus Garvey, Martin Luther King, Abraham Lincoln, Ghandi, Nelson Mandela, John F. Kennedy, Robert Kennedy, John Lennon, Muhammad Ali, Akala, Benjamin Zephaniah, Manny Pacquiao, Dave Chappelle, Chris Rock, Katt Williams.

Nelson Mandela School, Oldknow School, Waverley School, Touch of Class Boxing Gym, Birmingham City Boxing Club, Pat Benson Boxing Academy, Redbridge College, City of Westminster College, Staffordshire University, Staffordshire University Boxing Club, Stuart Sourbutts, Pete Tapper-Gray, ST1, Queensberry Police ABC, Impact ABC, Peacocks Gym, Bankside Health Club, Andre Olley, Hans Arnold, The Boxing Academy Hackney, Urban Warriors Academy, Duncan Eastrbrook, Stonebridge Boxing Club, Steve Goodwin, Kevin Campion, Josh Goodwin, Brian Gee, State of Mind Fitness, Barry O' Connell.

Believe

Believe

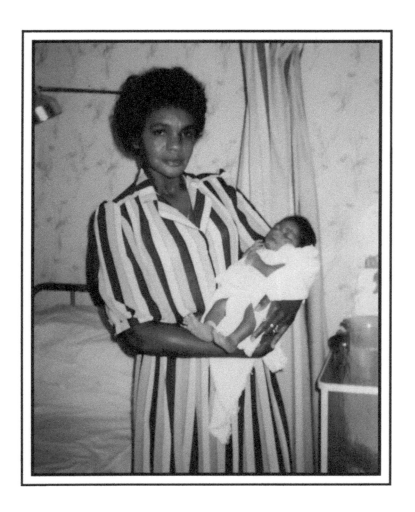

Believe

Believe

Believe

Believe

Believe

Believe

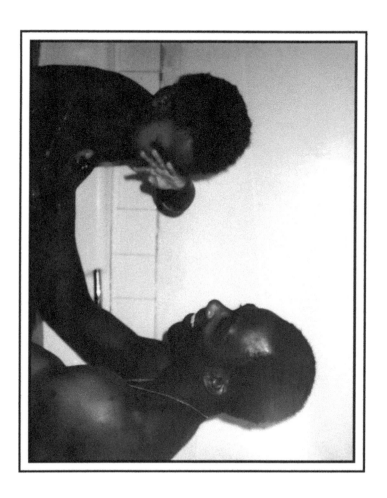

Believe

Believe

Preface

My Dad, a former professional boxer, introduced me and my older brother to boxing. We learnt the basics but were soon deterred by the distractions of teenage life.

I returned to boxing as a man, at Staffordshire University Boxing Club towards the end of 2005. My sole goal was to lose my beer belly. I explicitly told Ian Smith the coach that I did not want to spar or fight, my only purpose was to get fit. The coach and fellow boxers enhanced my confidence and fed my ambitious nature. In 2008, I made my amateur debut representing 'Queensberry Police ABC' in Stoke on Trent, winning via 2nd round TKO.

To date, in my current field as a professional boxer, I have had 13 fights and been victorious in 11, managing to win a Southern Area Title and be ranked in the Top 10 of the country.

Pressure coincides with my profession; most people around me only see the finale – me stepping into the ring, in great physical shape and performing well under the lights and cameras. Amidst the occasion, it is easy to assume that everything is fine.

There were certain points on this journey where, like most, my mental health has been tested but I did not express this to family. Instead, I found a way to remedy my emotional conflicts by myself, through poetry. Self-expression is essential for one's own wellbeing and in this current climate where we are becoming increasingly aware of Mental health, I believe that expressive forms such as poetry, have the power to be natural remedies.

I began writing in 2001.

At sixteen, I had to leave my home city of Birmingham for London as my Mum married. I left Small Heath Birmingham reluctantly; low and angered, no friends, completely new surroundings.

It was whilst resting in my Step dad's office, lying on a bed that was bought purposefully for me, that I wrote my first poem: an angry one full of obscenities.

Believe

As I matured, I learnt to transfer my thoughts into poems loud and clear minus the profanities. My experiences grew alongside the topics and depth. On that account, I decided to categorise each piece of poetry according to the era they were created.

The Old Chronicles (TOC) is a title that was ascribed to my earlier scribes. Although the message is pure, the delivery is significantly more unpolished. I wanted it to be authentic hence why the grammatical flaws and language errors were not corrected. I believe that this better characterises my earlier tales, some of which still remain valuable expressions in their own right.

The New Chronicles (TNC) unearthed a ripened style and wider diction that accompanied the huddle of enhanced tests and feelings which I have tussled with more recently and like both Chronicles, subjects that would have otherwise remained undisclosed were it not for the publication of this book.

Poetry helps me express myself to myself and is very therapeutic to me. A form of release that allows me to identify with greater scrutiny what exactly the underlying issue is. When I share poems and discover I am not the only one who has felt that way or gone through such situations, I gain a sense of achievement and purpose. To hear my words have soothed, triggered an emotion or memory is the biggest compliment I can receive as a poet.

Believe

T.I.S.S.U.E.S

Poetry is...

Concealer when my heart is winter to you I confide
Then expose when what is froze has been rectified

My narration report or survey
Certain scenes I replay
Celebration contemplation and dismay

That laugh cry insight
Thought it will trigger
Interpretation of how things function in my inner
Like wearing a white shirt in reverse
Revealing aspects clean and of dirt

Self-diagnosis when I am hopeless
Can't bench press the pain
Stationary shoulders until I focus elevating again and again
Surpassing my limitations to mental strain

My conjoined twin combined within
Or by page and pen
An angel guardian
My infinite flow friend
My fixation My opinion
Key to opening doors
My queries and conclusions
Recommendation in settling scores

Inhale exhale blink or shiver
That involuntary action when poetry I deliver

Voice
An identity which ranges
From the system's conspires
My desires
To He Who Is Due All Praises

My Sayonara, farewell
As I lay in the grave
Insurance I shall live on
Through every page

Believe

The Old Chronicles
(TOC)

Believe

Behind the Lines: Life's Prey
TOC

The innocence and purity we possess as a child inevitably diminishes. Some decisions we make as teens and adults do not mirror the superior IQ we have accumulated since the naivety of our childhood. With some of our decisions it is almost a certainty we would have made better choices as an infant. I for sure can place myself in that bracket. The weights we all carry, the scars we conceal can transform a certain 'no' into a 'maybe' or 'yes' tolerating a situation or instigating one when deep down within us clarity is denied the opportunity to manifest.

Believe

Believe

Life's Prey

Write a letter to my cousins locked in the pen
Reminisce of the days way back when...
That bouncing castle or playing in Nan's garden
Wishing now was more like then
We'd never think of a crime
Our freedom to sacrifice
But you like many became a victim of life...

Didn't realise her worth
Raised by her grandparents from birth
Felt unwanted until along came her 'first'
Gave her heart at the start he was so nice
He hit you once then it turned to twice
Cry, lie then push to the side
Because he 'cared' unlike all other guys
For love you thought that was the price
You too became a victim of life

Watching his Mother growing up she showed so much might
Single parent family money was tight
Grudge with the world never had what they wanted
So those who did... He targeted
Throw his hood up in them alleys on the darkest night
Placing food on the table felt wrong but right
He used to be content just riding around on his bike
Until he became a victim of life

Walked a rigid road upbringing always cold
So she fell instead of rose
Drugs helped her past memories erase
Gets high but never elevates
Alien to dressing up as she'll just dress down
They laugh as she roams around
Her story so far has been of pain and strife
Sadly, becoming a victim of life

Don't make the hard times reason for decline
But the cause of your success
Let life get the better of you? You get the best
Exchange that stage of struggle for an example of strength
And your downfall you could prevent

Believe

Behind the Lines: If I Changed the World
TOC

I was made aware of the great men and women who devoted their lives to making a positive change in the world as I was growing up - many of whom lost their lives in the process. Martin Luther King, Ghandi, Malcolm X, President Kennedy and Abraham Lincoln to name a few.

Through studying their objectives and the manner of their deaths, it was easy to associate changing the world positively with murder or assassination. In some cases, their death brought more attention to their life resulting in the power of their message growing significantly when they were no longer here in the flesh to witness.

Believe

31

Believe

If I Changed the World

If I did change the world...
History tells me I'd end up dying
Sacrifice my life for yours...
Still the evil will be targeting
If I'm the cause of a change
Begin to count my last days
Whether killed by my own people
Or assassinated with the infra-ray
I'd fall into God's arms
And tell him
"It's OK...
It's a shame the world had to do me this
way
I tried to increase their faith in you
And their will not to stray
Hope my deeds were good enough to enter heaven..."
I'll pray

If I did change the world
Would I even get to witness the result?
Would I be met with much laughter
And plenty insults?
I wonder would it take the attention
Of my un-timed fatality
For my words and work to be looked upon
And remembered seriously?

Believe

Behind the Lines: I Love You Mother
TOC

Like a lot of my poems from The Old Chronicles I look back at
my use of vocabulary and cringe at times but I always admire the
intention, the story.

This is possibly the oldest poem I have to show, the first to not
include any swearing (as I was showing it to my Mum) I gifted
this to her on her birthday in 2002, framed and handwritten. Slang
included (respect my stages).

33

Believe

Believe

I Love You Mother

I know I don't say this often
But you know that you're loved and…
God making you my mother was truly a blessing
And I would do anything to prevent you being put in a coffin
I know that you would do the same for me
One of the reasons my love for you was not created
It came naturally

Back in the day times were hard and appreciation? I didn't show it
But I'm trying my hardest now, to be thankful and considerate
You guided me through life
Without u I wouldn't have a clue
But there remains one thing I'll never be sure of…
What I would do without u

When I moan and complain, don't take to heart what I'm saying
My way of remaining sane:
Letting things out, instead of keeping them locked in the brain
I also hope you know I would never hurt you intentionally
But for the times I have, you must know I regret greatly
In a world full of fakes and people who pretend to be true
There's one person I can guarantee total sincerity from
And it's you

So thank you mum for your assistance and guidance through life
You have all the qualities I hope to find in a wife
On closing this poem
I apologise 4 anything I've done wrong in the past and for the
future
If you remember anything from this poem make sure it's
'I love you Mother'

On a list of importance to me, you are Number One
I mean every word in this poem. D. Mendes. Your Son

Believe

Behind the Lines: Reverse Order
TOC

One of my oldest surviving Poems. Written in 2003. I had left
Birmingham 2 years previously, I did my best to maintain all
relationships left behind, visiting as much as possible. I was
leaning towards the realisation that my peer group seemingly
found a greater satisfaction in mine or anyone else's wrong
doings. They were entertained by the very things I was now
shying away from participating in and some found mockery in the
developments I had made. My loyalty and common sense were in
conflict.

Believe

Reverse Order

Different from most, best describes me
Raised well but still didn't stop this sad story
How come the good guy always finishes last?
I'm tired of the norm but it won't knock me of my path
Why when I try to progress
To some I'm seen as a sinner?
When I learn from my mistakes I'm looked on as amateur?
What would they say, if I said I pray?
Would my ratings be the same?
As, if I told my friends I had seen my enemy
And put a bullet to his brain?
Why is it I get more respect for the wrong I do
And they look down on the right?
Aren't these the people I need to filter out my life?

Believe

Behind the Lines: Eyes of the System
TOC

Seated on a train reading a newspaper which had a short article
on CCTV. It detailed that we were recorded at least 300 times a
day. As a child of the 80's growing up in Birmingham this was a
statistic that surprised me. It led me to wonder who was watching
those in power. Those behind the desk making crucial decisions
that are shaping the population's future drastically. The ones
watching us are more of a liability yet the camera is always
facing the other way. What about them I ask. Transparency.

Believe

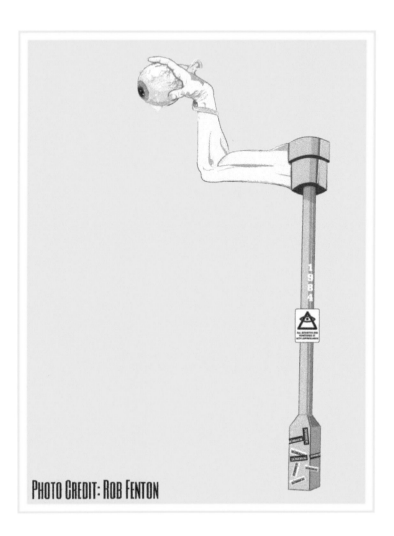

PHOTO CREDIT: ROB FENTON

Believe

Eyes of the System

Step out my house
And straight away
They can see
The eyes of the system
Constantly watching thee
Hanging from the post or stuck to the wall
Some you don't see
Impossible to dodge them all

Watched by the system an average 300 times a day
Wonder who's watching them who watch us and get paid
If my every move you're able to view
I have a question; what about you?

While the government conspires and deceives
Things going on in the White House you wouldn't believe
Point the camera in the other direction
Then things will become clear
Like why life's a constant struggle to survive out here
What if everyone masked up, walked the city streets
I'd smile that day, the cameras we'd defeat

Who's watching you while you're watching me?
Surely, you're the one capable of a greater catastrophe

Believe

Behind the Lines: A Dream of Death
TOC

I have frequently felt my life was of no value. Whether I lived or died was unimportant, I would often say, 'I'm good to go' in reference to my death. I still have the occasional bout where I feel nonchalant about my life span but this actual dream served as a temporary reminder I wasn't through yet.

Believe

A Dream of Death

Last night I had a dream, where in it I died
Sitting at the back of the bus
My final ride
Struggling to breathe I die in silence, so nobody cried
Everything shut down, except my sight and my mind...

Until my fatality I was sure I was ready to go
Sitting here reflecting on life...Now?
I don't know
As it seems all I'm doing is regretting
The good has been outnumbered by the sinning...

That's when it happened
A lady in front of me put her hand on my chest
Resurrected
God gave me breath
Followed by a gush of vomit
It kept going like a hose pipe
The beginning of my new life...

Then I awoke grateful I wasn't 6-feet under
With a chance to change myself for the better

See, I had to die to really realise
Got to be a worthy servant of you God
When eventually I demise

Appreciating it was a dream and not reality
Time for me to be the best I can be

Believe

Behind the Lines: Contradictions
TOC

Advice, quotes and references you'll find in abundance. Some
individuals bombard you with their code beseeching a
conversion. If we were to follow every righteous teaching we
would be served with contradictions and confusion. I address that
and drop my solving.

Believe

Contradictions

If I fought fire with water?
Eventually I'd be steaming
If I matched fire with fire?
It'd destroy everything
Live my life like a door mat or continuously sin?
Got me feeling like I can't win

'He who has knowledge...Has power'
But Aeschylus reported 'He who learns, must suffer'
Is truth when they say: 'Knowledge is key?'
Then why do I think if I knew it all that would be the death of
me?
Ironically my sanity would be the topic of discussion
Either accept with pride or crumble at the burden?

Jesus said 'Turn the other cheek' but then you're left with one
Could a wife or child be satisfied with this protection?
Adopt 'An eye for an eye' as my policy
Though you'd become blind says Ghandi
If I keep switching cheeks, they'll ruin my sight and my grin
Got me feeling like I can't win

'If you can't beat them, you'd better combine?'
I'm in a losing battle, I often find
So should I join forces with the wickedest mind?
Instead I step into the light that is My Guide

Everything done with noble intent is justified
This the motto to which I abide

Believe

Behind the Lines: Most Niggaz
TOC

This is potentially my most controversial poem. The use of the 'N' word may trigger many. I debated with myself whether to include this, though I knew if I did, my 'Behind the Lines' explanation would have to be one of depth.

I was working part time at a nightclub as a glass collector whilst studying at college and doing my best to maintain ties with my Birmingham affiliates during the time I wrote this poem.

Written in 2003 I was still smoking weed daily, drunk most days and like many who live that lifestyle, I was unsatisfied. Due to only being involved part time in the shenanigans of Small Heath Birmingham, my mind was developing rapidly; my positioning outside of the box allowed me to peep in and out of an unproductive, destructive lifestyle, a luxury I didn't have before.

Sitting in B10 9BL through the smoke that was turning the ceiling yellow, I was beginning to see traits I wanted to distance myself from. During my night job at the club, looking at 'the party' from the outside, again I was beginning to see traits I wanted to distance myself from.

Returning home from a shift at Faces Nightclub I took out a pen and some paper, lay on my bed and completed 'Most Niggaz' - the first poem I wrote at my new flat having left my Step dad's house. I now resided in the East Ham area of London.

I have been heavily influenced by hip hop music; Tupac Shakur easily gained a holding on my playlist. My use of the word in this poem was not to degrade a particular race but describe people in general, a type of person that any race can be, the type of person that I can be and have been at various stages in my life.

Regardless of race: we all sin. What separates us though, is the ability to identify it and the urge to change those destructive

Believe

patterns of behaviour rather than embrace it and repeat it with no remorse or hesitation.

In recent years, I considered changing the controversial word to 'People' 'Dudes' or 'Fellas' but poetry is my reflection and those that read assumingly want to know my story, my poems are my story in its truest form, changing the content (to me) is deceit. This is who I was at the time and where I was (mentally) at the time. If you are not offended, I thank you and if you are, I apologise. I would ask you to kindly turn the pages to witness the progression in my writing through the use of language and change in attitude moving on from that point when I was just 19 years of age.

Believe

Most Niggaz

Most niggaz would kick an enemy when he's down
Most niggaz would underestimate the neighbourhood clown
Most niggaz would touch a hoe, if she opened up wide
Most niggaz would have a wife, plus a hoe on the side
Some niggaz would rob you then ask you 'who did it'
Some niggaz don't wanna stop the beef, they wanna encourage it
Some niggaz tell you it's good then tell their homie it's whack
Some niggaz tell you over and over 'I got your back'
Some niggaz is rollin with you cus they got a hidden agenda
Maybe they like your girl, or they think you got loads of paper

See there's a lot of niggaz like all the above who I despise
But we aren't all like this, try not to generalise
See at times, we all slip into a bad category
We aren't perfect;
The important thing is realising that's not what you wanna be

I wanna be one of the few niggaz
And I know there's a few niggaz like me…

See few niggaz will look you in the face
And give you an honest opinion
Few niggaz see trouble coming
And remove themselves from that situation
Few niggaz will leave their enemy to live their own life
Few niggaz will move on, instead of sharpening the knife
Few niggaz wouldn't touch a hoe, 'cus few niggaz know better
Look through empty girls and don't even bother
Few niggaz is looking for a girl who deserves their all
Few niggaz is there for their people when they desperately call
You can look in the eyes of a few niggaz,
And know that they are real
Not always talking about this bitch they fucked,
How much money they got
Or this nigga they wanna kill

I wanna be one of the few niggaz
Hopefully we'll grow like tree
Turning few niggaz into most niggaz, gradually

Believe

Behind the Lines: My Responsibility
TOC

Frustrations sparked the rising of a pen in this instance as I was unable to grasp how many celebrities failed to address relevant topics. I couldn't figure out how people with such a huge following did little or nothing to build the consciousness of potentially millions that hang on their every word.

The highest profile celebrity on twitter, at the time of writing this has 107.23 million followers. The highest profile celebrity on Instagram has 244 million followers. Imagine if either of these celebrities recommended a book to their fan base that wasn't their biography. Imagine if they spoke up on racism, poverty, political deceit. Imagine if they recommend their followers complete at least one deed of righteousness, an unselfish act in his or her honour or gave daily talks of inspiration, encouragement and hope to their army.

I had reason to believe I was the only one with thoughts of this nature, here is my query to God.

Believe

My Responsibility?

Sometimes life itself may seem a misery
Check the murder rate
The extremes of poverty
Together we could make a difference
Instead they stare, blindly
Got me asking God questions
Stressing me, daily
I'm not the only one that can see?
But could it be?
To make a change in this world my duty, solely

I can't die in vain
Must make history
Join the ranks of Malcolm, Martin and Garvey
With you Lord by my side…
Sure, anything's a possibility
Dear God have you made to change the world
Just my responsibility?

Believe

Behind the Lines: A Thug's Tale
TOC

Living in the areas I lived in and having the friends I had, I was able to witness and experience some of the circumstances that lead to the opening line of this poem. Growing up poor is by no means an excuse to embrace a criminal life but it can enhance your level of desperation, luring you down that dark road.

Poverty is something I have lived at various stages of my life and referenced in various poems; it can damage physically, mentally and socially as I have found. If I could change one thing about the world we inhabit, it would be poverty.

Believe

A Thug's Tale

Another black youth pulled the trigger last night
They say we'll never break free of the stereotype
Easy to say, from the outside looking in
But when you're living in poverty it isn't hard to sin

Remember watching Mother as she followed the rules
I was a youth
She never broke a law but struggled to raise us
Government not speaking the truth
Me like many other wanted a different route
Surrounded by people who walked in similar boots...

Became friends got to know one another
Wanted success in this life
Seen the system as failure

We'd meet up, get high, again and again
Only way we knew how to bring pleasure from pain
Parents not aware, so no place to go except the street corner
Media got it confused, labelled it all 'gang culture'
When discussions of the struggle often consumed time
A solution, the future - were topics on our mind

"I wana become a teacher"
"That will take at least 5 to 6 years"
"We could make money right now if we sold this right here"

Once you choose that path, it's hard to reverse
Try change your life
Maybe you'd get killed, or have your face in the dirt
Tempers fly, you could meet jail or death with a feeling of regret
Living in a place where money is hard to get
They cling onto something free
Their pride and respect

Reducing poverty should be the government's principal target
Instead inflation each year, they're doing the opposite
So supporters of the system we find it hard to be
Life's not a curse but it's worse in a poor community

51

Believe

Behind the Lines: Sanction My Portrayal
TOC

'Sanction my Portrayal' is my appeal to God, my call on Him to share my vision and implement it. Aware my words are powerless in the grand scheme of things, this poem serves as a pointless plea yet a remedial fantasy. Where in the peak of my imagination reading this poem can bring temporary alleviation as I transport myself to the 'ideal world' I speak of.

As I ventured out of The Old Chronicles my approach to writing was maturing, lines and stanzas were becoming less clear cut, some would require decoding or a gentle nudge in the right direction.
'Civilisation meets The Mother' (The Motherland, Africa in its entirety)

Believe

Sanction My Portrayal

Dear God talk to me
Can you tell me a story?
Of how my life maps out
So I don't need to worry
Please reassure me…
I'm going to live comfortably
Set up home where love is shown throughout my family
Won't you come talk to me?...

Put your hand on my shoulder
Say:
   'The struggle is not to be a part of my Great Grand kid's future'

Promise they'll discover a cure for my people of Africa
There's end to the suffer, civilization meets The Mother

Tell me:
       'War is soon to become like a myth from the past'

We can't believe it happened because we got peace at last
I hear people will stop thinking just of self
The rich wised up, learnt where to channel their wealth
So there's an answer to the millions that remain poor
Some don't turn to crime in desperation no more

Then can you look me in the eyes, tell me it's true…
Demise to child murder, assaults and abuse
The streets are no longer the stage for coldness, lack of mercy
Crime was the past, the future is peace, harmony

I beg as our conversation reaches its finale
You say…

 'When your heart completes its last beat, there's no need to worry
     You and your loved ones go ever so peacefully
       To be amongst me is your destiny'

Believe

Behind the Lines: I've Grown
TOC

'I've Grown' was my evaluation on the latest developments within my character, written within a couple days of another transitioning poem, 'Most Niggaz.' I was 19 years old, still writing in slang, please forgive the informal language and appreciate the message.

Believe

I've Grown

Feeling Different nowadays, guess D's becoming a man
Things I can't do no more. My friends? They won't understand
Touching random girls with no hesitation
I'm not going to sleep with no one if there is no emotion
No longer all about the breast and the bumper
All's needed is a pretty face
Someone I'll feel proud introducing to Mother

Now there's a whirlwind of thoughts spinning in my mind...
Thinking which one should I pull out and put in a rhyme
When I was young... had so many friends, well at least I thought
Now I'm rolling solo daily
Fully independent, everything D has D bought
20 soon, basically my teens are over
It's about discipline now, knowing your border
Becoming a changed man without struggle there is no progress In
order for us to learn we must first go through the stress

Trying not to complain remember what I have instead of what I
need
Finally realised the importance of my family
When D was younger, he just wanted Mum to leave him alone
Wanted to do as I pleased, as if I was grown
But now I hesitate to put down the phone
Don't feel awkward any more to say "I love my Mother" Thank
her for my upbringing and I will owe her forever

I'm calmer now; believe It's for the better
However my friends, they beg to differ
They tell me I'm weak but I'm knowing I'm stronger
Having bigger dreams now it's not about the money and the
power I want: A woman to love and eventually a family of my
own to look after
Do less wrong and do more right
Peace of mind when walking the streets, on the darkest night

Going to close this now, I think what's in my mind has been
shown
What I'm trying to say here is "Damn it! I've grown"

Believe

Behind the Lines: Out of the Ghetto
TOC

Relocating to London took me out of my comfort zone and moving to Stoke-on-Trent to begin University (where I subsequently began boxing again) I ventured even further away from familiar surroundings with regards to my peer group. On many occasions I felt out of place, like I shared no common ground with my new associates. I became even more muted in my new environment. I was reluctant to share my experiences or mentality. Unsurprisingly whenever I detected someone of a similar background or mind-set, I came out of my shell with ease. Shying away from social gatherings was my solution but the stubbornness in me wasn't willing to accept that remedy permanently. I was aware I needed to add new dimensions to my character repertoire.

Sitting at a computer in Staffordshire University Library, Mr Robert Fenton, someone who I had met at the University's Boxing Club, invited me to NYC. He reeled off all of the names of my possible fellow holiday makers, following the last name he mentioned, the first thing I had already concluded... I was going to be the only black guy there. My immediate internal response was 'forget that, no way am I going' but then I recalled my intention, the need to develop. Following that reassessment, the same reason I had for not wanting to go became my reason to go. It was a great holiday, so great we ended up going again and Rob became a permanent figure in my small yet solid circle of friends.

Believe

Believe

Out of the Ghetto

Mom loved me, school my only worry
Wish I could take it back to how it was
It started when we left Pops and I grew with plenty thugs
Looked after by the wolves
Grew my claws
Registered that life in my mind everything stored
A child baptised by the thugs and dealers
Did what they do
Walked in their shoes
Regular clash of tempers
Unstable however comfortable within this life
Question me about the streets? No need to think twice

But who would have thought my life would change like so
Beginning with my departure out of the ghetto
A deer blinded by the headlights or even a black sheep
Been scarred by my surroundings, it got me soul deep
Battling against the tide I know I'm not complete
There are still many characteristics I'd like to achieve
Like a baby that's new to the game
My soul a raging bull I'm trying to tame
An adopted child getting use to his new family
Or a foreigner trying to adjust to a new country
Put simply…

Amongst 'Good People' it's hard to mingle
Ashamed to say amongst the hustlers is where I'm most
comfortable
What am I to do, can't settle for less
Come a long way, in this unpredictable test
Changed many ways, left certain people at the gate
Still amongst the dogs, feel I can always relate
And when among the righteous, struggle to conversate
You know what they say
'Rome wasn't built in a day'
I just wonder how long this transition will take
I'll pray
        "God please help me change my ways;
        It wasn't my choice for this it's how I was raised"

Believe

Behind the Lines: Lost
TOC

My initial brush with depression as a man came in my first year at University. I met someone that unintentionally lowered my IQ with ease. Besotted, I plunged into a relationship swiftly. Being young, irresponsible and in love a pregnancy followed. With us both being freshmen and having worked so hard to get to University, I told my partner, 'whatever you decide, I support your decision, you will have to leave your studies, not me.'

I wrote this poem whilst being in limbo about her decision, at a time when communication was lacking on both sides. I was working and studying, present but absent at the same time. Lost.

Believe

Lost

A time when I'm lost for words
Running short of laughter
I'm finding it hard to deal with the stress
My shoulders can't take the pressure
A time the closest people to me
Seem the furthest away
Because I've got to deal with this alone
In my mind it's the only way
So I force a smile and tell them "I'm OK"
Sit in my box with my soul mates; me, myself and I
Listening to the tunes that have been a soundtrack to my life
A time I question my sanity
Am I crazy?
What do you figure?
Do I need a cushioned room, with cameras behind the mirror?
So what do I do now?
I've already prayed
God called me a stranger so now I'm talking to this page

Believe

Behind the Lines: Lost Pt 2
TOC

Following my partner's indecisiveness, she seemingly abruptly changed her mind and chose to abort. The circumstances of the abortion broke me as I had accepted I was going to be a Father. She was the first partner of mine to meet my family, My Father, Nan, (late Grandad etc. She was introduced to them, we announced our new arrival, she then visited London to see her Mother (RIP) and called me days later saying she had had a late abortion. I was silenced. We ended our crash course of a relationship, my weed addiction escalated worryingly. I was also 'getting drunk' as I wrote this, alone in my shared university accommodation room.

Believe

Lost Pt 2

365 days
12 months
One whole year
Since I lost what I should have had so I'm shedding this tear
'There's nothing more precious than life'
That's what they say
So why did I have to treat yours that way?
Was I high too young or just selfish
What I would do right now if I had one wish
I'd look in your eyes
I imagine they were just like mine
Hold you
Feed you and 'shush' you when you were cryin
When you got big we'd play ball I wonder if you could dunk
Instead I'm sitting here
Holding a pen
Getting drunk
It could have been me and you against the world
But I chose me so what I'm going through I guess I deserve
Blaming myself
My desire for perfection
Did I really want a baby with her?
Was she 'the one?'
I'll remember you always
But you? Forget about me son
Your father was a fool please forgive me for what I've done
And I pray some day we'll meet
In heaven

Believe

Behind the Lines: Operation: Equality
TOC

Written and performed for a diversity themed night on the campus of my University. A rare occasion I was asked to write a poem for something specific and obliged. John Lennon's - 'Give Peace a Chance' helped to close this declaration.

Believe

Operation: Equality

Blessed with a heart beat
Gift from The One above
All trying to make it in this world
That often seems tough
We love laughter and cry when felt necessary
And smile at the face of a new born baby

To different tunes we tap our feet
Various languages we may speak
Our selection of interests and opinions
Are what makes us unique

Though some would prefer a world with everything similar
Guarantee we'd still find time to war with another
There's some bad people out there
Be sure, no one's superior
They say don't judge a book
Without checking the interior

Picture a world with one type of clothing
Similar music beats
Only a small range of food possible to eat
Pray one day all of us can see
How boring it would be without diversity

Some say a peaceful society is simply asking too much
It can't be promised, it's neither fact or bluff
Potential to forever remain a mystery
Until we start trying hard enough

Believe

Behind the Lines: Comfort in You
TOC

I found myself preferring female company as I drifted away physically and mentally from many of my longest standing friends. The boisterous, reckless and at times confrontational behaviour from my male peer group was becoming draining and problematic. My time at Staffordshire University forced me away from such a crowd. I was able to identify a new tranquillity spending time with females where 'the guard' was unnecessary, the charade was unnecessary, I could be me and it would be received well, free from mockery and insult. 'Comfort in You' was my first piece of three dedicated to a type of female that has been a key figure in my development.

Believe

Comfort in You

Why is it when the day is through
Life seems blue
The only comfort I find is within you
Whether it's the look in your eyes
Your voice or being in the same room
As long as you're around I know comforts coming soon
A lion out the cage the only one that can tame
Conversation with the boys could never be the same
An addiction in my life I'm not ashamed to claim
Without you I'd be like a dog off the chain
What I'm saying...
Sitting in a group or alone on a park bench
Without you in my life I wonder how I would see sense
Talking about my partner I am not
This so much more you see
Throughout my life you've put out the flame that often ignites in D
The type of bond in my heart
No need for touch or lust
Found from city to city
But still I can't have enough
Many have departed from my life but still never fear
I've been blessed with a number of sources for this love right here
So we can lay on my bed or talk on the phone
Still waiting for the one I'll see every time I come home
This link I refer to if you have not guessed already
Is the soothing of my heart when in the presence of a lady

Believe

Behind the Lines: Mail
TOC

9 family members in jail at one time - that statistic was my
reality. Writing frequently and visiting on occasions was a loving
yet heart-breaking experience. When the prison guard would
come over and tell you that your time is up it hit me on a
different level. I was distinctly aware of the fact that I was going
outside to experience my freedom and they were going back to a
cell which was an inevitable reality but still a tragic end to my
visits every time.

I wrote this to my cousin while he was incarcerated and sent it to
him along with a routine letter.

Believe

Mail

(Dedicated to Junior Edwards 'Stranger')

Wasup Cus it has been along time since me and you spoke
Come to think of it
We haven't spoken in years
Just wrote
But trust it's the same shit going on out here
These niggaz claiming to be real when they're not even near

Still waiting for the day you finally get free
That will be one more nigga I could roll street with comfortably
Knowing I'm there for you like you're there for me
That shits hard to do out here so many mans be phony

Still no closer to completing my mission
To make a change in this world of deception and confusion
It's like every time I push forward
The system be pulling me back
Dreamt of a happy ending but it's hard to track
Things are tougher for us blacks and that's a fact
The struggle can touch us all though;
The story of many where you are at
I could go on forever about how this world be cold
But I'd just be telling you things you already know

But Cus that's me
It's my time to go
I'm a keep strolling on until the end of the road
Soon we'll meet
Until then you do you and I'll do me
Anything you need I'll do my best
We family

Believe

Behind the Lines: Waitin 4 D 1
TOC

Heartbreak from Lost Pt1/2 had me on a voluntary hiatus from any sexual relations. I had been so deep in love for the first time. The level of the betrayal affected my ability to move on. For a period of 12 months, I abstained from intercourse, the dust had to settle. I had to be as sure as possible that my next venture would not end the same way. I still believed in love, I was just waiting, waiting for 'The One'.

Believe

Waitin 4 D 1

What can I say what can I do about the reason I be stressing?
I'm missing a female in my world to enjoy life's blessing
Where's she at?
I pray God sends her quick
Until then I have only myself to confide with
So what am I to do with this love I refuse to through away?
What if I meet my future wife, I may need it that day
It's like pulling back a dog and he just wants you to let go
Or a dam that's restricting the water flow
What it feels like to have unconditional love for someone
I've got to know
Wish it was as easy as lighting a candle
Making a wish
Then blow
If so, I'd wish for a perfect wife and to watch my seeds grow
Gaze into my wife's eyes amazed, and say:

"Look, look what we've done"
"God has blessed us with a beautiful daughter and son"

Believe

Behind the Lines: I'll Pray
TOC

Sometimes we encounter people who have been positioned specifically to deliver a message and then depart. Anthea Cox was that person for me.

I met her at a Brazilian Carnival that used to take place near Angel, London. I was still avoiding any form of romance. Me and my good friend Simeon had stepped out of an Off license holding a mini bottle of wine each. Simeon was quick to point out that we had gained the attention of a group of females standing opposite. I reminded him I was still 'on strike' from women, following my previous relationship and Simeon proceeded to position his mouth beside my ear and repeatedly question my sexuality. I caved in; we walked over.

My attention initially went to a lady in the group that was not Anthea, Simeon was prompt in redirecting me to the petit, mixed-race, South African. As soon as we began talking the topic of conversation wasn't small talk, or chat up lines, Anthea asked me if I believed in God, intrigued I said, "Yes."
She continued, "With all the time you probably spend listening to music, watching TV, playing computer games do you ever put aside any time to say thank you?" I said, "No" and immediately wanted to change that. We exchanged numbers and she invited me to her church.

Over a short time, we spent a lot of time together. I used to dress in 3XL t-shirts and sweaters that hung as low as my knees. I was smoking weed daily. Anthea made very clear her disapproval which we would laugh and joke about.
She was a strong lady of faith so sexual advances were non-existent between the two of us in the absence of marriage.

I eventually accompanied her to church. I was without spiritual direction, but never without my phone, keys, wallet, weed, grinder, rizla and tobacco, which I had in my pocket entering church.

Believe

The sermon consisted of a story. The pastor was supervising at a Christian Camp where one of the children attending challenged him to a race.

The pastor boasted to the attendees of the congregation that when he was in school, he was the fastest runner, athletic and sporty, he relayed this to the child who challenged him and footed the line confident of victory. The child beat him. At that point, The Pastor realised as gifted as he was as a child, he didn't nurture it and his gift soon passed him by. The pastor pleaded with us not to let our gift escape us, whether it is spiritual, physical or mental.

I sat and reflected. I too was extremely sporty in school, the fastest runner in my Primary and Secondary school from 100 to 800m. Captain of my secondary school basketball team and a prominent member of the school's football team. The Pastor's words rang home. I had neglected everything I was ever good at. Boxing was a mere pastime. Upon leaving the church, I threw away my weed, rizla, cigarettes and kept the grinder which I later gave to my aunty. I never smoked weed again.

Believe

I'll Pray (*Anthea Cox*)

Wounded by the drama
To God I prayed
First I begged for his mercy on me on Judgement Day
My guilty conscience picturing me going up in a blaze
So I pleaded for him to help me change my ways
As He's The Almighty and to Him we must praise
Finally fed up making mistakes and tired of the games
Asked for my next relationship to last until the end of my days
Then I blew onto my hands and in bed I laid…

Temptations came along but still I never strayed
Then along came a lady capable of taking me to the next stage
Blessed with wisdom from above
Natural beauty so unique
I felt God was on my side the way he made us meet
The window to her soul her eyes so deep
Made every last one of my defences weak

Could this be, the answer to my prayers?
Since we've met
I've stopped a bad habit I have been working on for years
Whether by my side permanently
Or temporary like a cool summers breeze
I still thank God for the revelation as I bow my head on my knees
Besides Mom never before has someone graced my life in such a
way
I do hope it's just the beginning
Every night
I'll pray

Believe

Behind the Lines: A Poem for Pops
TOC

My Father fathered many but we love him no less. He wasn't a prominent figure like my Mother. No, we didn't see him often but the time we spent he would use productively. No shortage of advice, sharing his experiences and speaking with passion when instructing us to aim high and not fall victim to the temptations that would hamper our acceleration.

The intention behind this was to print, frame and gift for Father's Day, ideally, I wanted all 10 of us siblings to contribute lyrically, I failed, though I believed my words spoke for us all.

Believe

Believe

A Poem for Pops

A lot of the time Mothers take all the credit
Fathers don't get a mention
This
From the heart
Is our dedication

Growing up we didn't see you often
Now I realise you were out trying to make ends meet
Why my first memory of you was coming in the room
Whilst you was asleep
Every now and then we'd go out with cousins' sisters and brother
These are the scenes of my childhood I value and treasure

Forget never
When we were much younger
Drove us to the ghetto pointed out the addict prostitute and dealer
Preached we should aim to accomplish much more in life
Like a seed planted in our minds was your advice

Told us stories of your past
At times it was tragic
But you overcame all obstacles
Accepting no excuse as valid

For our upbringing, what you continue to do, we'll always admire
So Father's Day insignificant, as we'll never fail to remember
How you want for us to have
What you never...
A friend in a Father who stepped up
Never retreated
A busy man but is continuously there
Whenever needed

A true definition of a Father, a figure to aspire to
Happy Father's Day Pops we all love you

Believe

Behind the Lines: Carry the Name
TOC

At this stage in my life, with my permanent exclusion from
Secondary School, I knew what it felt like to be a disappointment
to the family. I was adamant that I was going to turn things
around. I was months into my cannabis free lifestyle which gave
me a different energy and outlook on life. The cloud of smoke was
clearing and my optimism was revealing itself. On reflection, this
was my last poem in which any potentially offensive language was
used.

Believe

Photo Credit: Kraize Kat

Believe

Carry the Name

Locked in solitude
Shoulders bearing the pain
I'm carrying all my family's expectations
Can't damage the name
So I'll return from my journey carrying the torch with the flame
Showing proof it's possible for a hood nigga to gain
Hoping others in my family will see and follow
If it didn't work that day there's always tomorrow
I puffed puffed and passed that spliff over for good
Been blazin since 13 so no one believed I could
The game was getting tough; had to sharpen my brain
Put my fate in God's hands
Since then it hasn't been the same
Carrying the weight content
Because I know someone else's burden is worse
So I'll carry the name on my journey
Promise them I'm not going to burst
Just keep my heart clean by avoiding the dirt
Come the end of my travels
In my eyes you'll find a success story
A man whose past was so dim
But his future's filled with glory

Believe

Behind the Lines: I Promise if I Make it
TOC

During a time of self-realisation, I discovered I wanted to make a difference with my life. I felt boxing was the most likely source of me doing so. This was written shortly before my amateur debut (pictured). I had worked hard and changed my life. This poem was not only my promise to everyone I feel had earned my loyalty at the time but also my promise to the strangers in society whose lives I felt I could contribute to positively.

'The struggle' has been a daunting, monotonous figure throughout my life, to relieve as many as I can of that burden, most notably those without a home is an urge I have within.

Believe

Believe

I Promise if I Make it

I promise if I make it I won't forget who put me in this place
Fall to my knees and praise God The Most Great
Thank Him for yet another gift He has given to me
Promise I won't abuse it, but use it responsibly

I promise if I make it I'll embrace my Mom
Rest my head on her shoulder
Thank her again for my life and tell her the struggle is over
My pops, thanks for sending me boxing when I was young in the
game
Got a big position for you; I want you involved in my fame
Whenever wherever I rep the family name
Tell my brother "stop chasing that paper"
The raggy road we once walked has come to an end soldier
To my little brothers and sisters everything is going to be fine
Can't be content just me getting mine
So I'll make sure everyone of you shine

All my brethren that shown me much love in life
The ones selling the herb making beats or clutching the mic
You've got a piece of my heart
For you to not come up with me wouldn't be right
Everyone who greeted me with a smile or asked me
'How do you do?'
I wish I could locate you all and help you come up too

I promise if I make it I'll remain humble
Remember knowledge is key
Share the wisdom I've been blessed with internationally
To every area I've lived in, there's many, you know where you are
Wherever I am I represent the strugglers, 'til death do us part
I promise if I make it you won't see no ice around my neck
Nor pay no man to protect and my morals they will be kept
I promise if I make it I'll build homeless shelters across the globe...
There's so much I want to do, only The Lord knows

I promise if I make it I won't forget where I'm from
Disrespect any or forget about The Greater One

Believe

Behind the Lines: Blood Stains
TOC

I worked as a door supervisor whilst boxing as an amateur in Stoke-on-Trent and in London. It wasn't unusual to see bloodshed. During my years on the door, I had punched, been punched, seen stabbings, baseball bats pinging off of heads, the works. One night in particular there was a mass brawl outside Liquid Club in Hanley, Stoke-on-Trent. A puddle of blood remained after the melee.

During my run the following morning, I passed near the site of the bloodshed where I had been working only hours before. I saw a street cleaner tending to the now red stain on the floor. Equipped with a spray, he seemed to blast the blood stain out of the concrete.

The second verse was birthed out of the most upsetting incident I have ever witnessed in the flesh.
Myself, my older brother and old secondary school friend, Nathan Henry, sat in a restaurant with a window view of the street. Our plans following the meal were to go to the cinema to watch Transformers, The Movie (I believe).

Whilst dining we heard a crash. We turned to the window simultaneously, catching sight of a small body sliding along the road, seemingly in slow motion.
We all rushed outside to find a young boy lying unresponsive on the floor, immediately we called '999'. A man we assumed was the child's father chased (on foot), captured and physically attacked the driver. The driver would then break free and run away but it was inevitable that he had to return to the scene and await police questioning. On his return to the harrowing scene he would again, understandably be met with the wrath of the motionless child's father. This cycle repeated itself throughout the whole ordeal.

The boy's head had swollen to indescribable measures, still fully immobilized. The ambulance eventually came. My school friend, the only father amongst the three of us at the time said, 'I'm going home to see my kids,' instantly ending our day. My brother and I

Believe

were not critical of his sentiment. The incident will remain in our mind forever.

Following the accident, I checked the local news daily for any information on that tragic moment. It was reported that the child was in stable yet critical condition and the ambulance had received over 60 calls from the public in response.

I look back on that day with sorrow yet also respect for the other individuals there. 'Over 60 calls to the ambulance' - this was testament to a different era where in the face of a disaster or potentially fatal accident, people only took out their phones to call for help. A few years down the line this would change. Some were more likely to film your demise instead of make a call to prevent it.

Believe

Blood Stains

Drama in the street the victim's blood sprayed
Made a puddle on the concrete it was cleaned the next day
Soon it went from the front to back of our memory
Then on went the cycle of a troubled community
But what if the stains remained
To remind us of our fallen society

Road accident
Boy in critical condition car doing over 40
It happened fast... SMASH Then everything went slowly
The boy's silent pain
"There's got to be a change"
"Things can never be the same"
"People got to stop speeding in that damn bus lane"
But then they came... With this spray
Cleaned the blood away...
They speeding again
Like what happened
Didn't happen that day

Said by many; Malcolm X, Martin Luther to Bob Marley
What's needed in this world is peace and unity
'Fantasy is what we want, but reality is what we need'
That's what Ms Lauryn Hill preached
We need to clean up our heart before we clean the streets
If we have to see the blood until it covers all the floor
Maybe then it will touch us permanently to end this life long war

Believe

Behind the Lines: Wedding Prayer
TOC

On two occasions I was asked to write a poem for a wedding. One being my Sister's Janine Mendes, whose wedding I performed a version of this along with my sister's Maid of Honour, Natasha Trent (also a poet), who added some lyrics of her own. It was a beautiful day in Jamaica - a family occasion I am grateful to have experienced, also my first holiday with my Dad.

Believe

Believe

Wedding Prayer

You will look into each other's eyes and say "I do"
The only time when 1+1 does not equal 2
So with love
Patience
And the blessing of God to see you through
May this beautiful relationship forever continue
Endless pleasures
Life's challenges
Together you must endure
When one is ill…
The other becomes the cure
A unique combination of two you can't divide
An official declaration of commitment
Between groom and bride
So as the lord looks down
Smiling from above
Let us witness two people uniting as one
Forever in love…

Believe

Behind the Lines: 2 Destinations
TOC

One of my early attempts at a spiritual themed poem. My theory on life and it's objectives. The lesson of this existence. I coincidentally foretell my boxing name by labelling myself a 'servant' 8 years later the name D. Servant would be stitched on the front of my shorts, for the occasion of my professional boxing debut.

Believe

2 Destinations

Lean my head back
Pause
Take a deep breath
Try and remove the stress
Sometimes we have got to learn of someone else's tragedy
To realise that we're blessed
Heart still beating in my chest
Blood running through my vein
For everyone reading it's the same
So let's give thanks for another day
Instead of moan and complain
My life's not mine to live
It is a gift I treat it as a loan
God gave me the keys to his car…
Told me 'find your way home'
We've all got him in us
Look deep inside
Discover the soul
The voice that says 'don't do it'
Will you do as you're told?
Or listen to the insincere voice
It wants you to burn like coal
Instead to rest in heaven with the Lord
Is my number one goal So who am I?
Or more relevantly who are we?
My answer is whatever we choose to be
Hopefully I'm a friend to you
Sure a servant to the Lord above
I'm about a positive change and spreading plenty love
Next time you're out look at the sky, the birds…
All His beautiful creations
Ask yourself when you die
(Heaven or hell) your choice of two destinations?
Now is it deserved? Be honest people
Judging by your actions…

Believe

Behind the Lines: Green Daze
TOC

At this point it was just over a year since I had quit smoking cannabis, like a disgruntled ex I spoke of my previous relationship, the fondness and the regret. Finding myself once the weed had left my system. My drug use had a strong hold over my decision making, memory and nerves. In the most simplistic of situations e.g. getting on a packed bus, I couldn't do it. I lacked confidence, ambition and all productive forms of enthusiasm.

Without the drug in my system I discovered a modified version of myself, wishing I had met him sooner.

Believe

Believe

Green Daze

You got piece of cigarette, what about blue Rizla?"
Reminiscent of my days as a chronic smoker
I was a youth
Before my deep voice
Before I had met a girl and gone through
I was holding you
Crumbling you and getting high with my crew...
Took you under my wing and together we grew

We had our ups and downs...
Laugh for hours and still serious topics we could debate
We had our anthems
Without you in my hand me and those tunes couldn't relate
My 21st Birthday I had a 1/2 ounce
My Dad brought a next one for his Son
Rolled up 13 spliffs and went to see Capleton
Me and you so many memories, that's just one...
Come to think of it, because of you, many memories are gone

When I was down I thought you helped, but no, you just delayed...
What I would have to wake up to and face the next day
From boy to man you've been in my blood
My true identity? It's unknown
We separated but I'm still coughing you up on a regular
Even when on the phone
The price I paid
You took my memory and in my body, made a home

It's been a year now since me and you played
I see you got some new friends; you don't care that I've strayed
Weed free I'm like a lion who feels he could have been stronger
But too many times I put you to my lips
And inhaled that tranquilizer

Believe

Behind the Lines: G's Team
TOC

My allegiance here had officially changed. the Title (G's Team) was a intentional play on words. Often the younger generation (as I did) find fascination in a lifestyle that is habitually glamorised albeit in music or movies, being a 'G' (gangster) is macho, respected, powerful.
My agenda in life changed, I found a alternative route, following a different 'G' code, a superior way, God's way, more macho, respected and powerful than any other way of life, the ultimate 'G'. I wanted to be sworn in.

I encountered blatant disapproval from some friends, telling me I was 'soft' 'feminine' had been 'brain washed' to name a few. Me calling time on my weed addiction prompted A friend to tell me I couldn't quit because 'weed is who you are'. Yes I felt alone, I made countless attempts for them to see through my lens, most unsuccessfully.

Believe

G's Team

Is there hope for all of us I wonder?
As success I see within my range
Wish I could spread like a virus
Pass on the urge for change
Blessed with direction, for this I must give praise
Travelled far from my stray old days
Grateful for eternity for everything you have shown
It's just I look around
See my close ones
Yet I'm alone

Tell them what I see but they don't agree
Their lifestyles will lead to regrets
Eventually
They will rob and steal saying it has to be done
But don't we each walk the path that we have
Chosen
Explain for me how it was and they want to tell me how it is
Look at me like I've just woken up from the seventies
Not seeing the relevance of my experiences
So my warnings
They fall on deaf ears
Flashbacks of my Father talking when I was sixteen years…

He would say:
"Forget your friends 'cus in the danger, they will step on your toes,
      you die like you came into this world, all on your own"

But I was deaf so how can I expect them to hear
Told the fire was hot but still I had to stand near
From a prayer had the veil removed dirt cleaned out my ear
It's like He answered me straight away did He see I was sincere
Now with each step I take only God I fear

He's like a coach and I'm trying to earn my place on the team
As long as I perform now he doesn't care where I've been

Believe

Behind the Lines: My Imaginary Lady (Grace)
TOC

'Grace' the illusion caused heartache when my girlfriend at the
time found the poem in my absence which was laying around in
my shared student accommodation room. She broke down in to
tears sobbing whilst attempting to speak clearly said "she is
nothing like me"
I cant remember the excuse I gave but it worked, she stayed with
me. I think a lot of us have an idea of what is our 'ideal', this
was mine in 2007.

Believe

My Imaginary Lady (Grace)

I think I have a problem
See I'm in love with this lady
She lives in my mind it's all imaginary...

Trying to increase my knowledge whilst in the library
Saw her there in the isle for black history
In a dress that hugged her body but kept her goods hidden
Moved in closer she had a lot of hair it was wrapped like a turban
God must be rewarding me for saying bye to my playa ways
She turned and said
"How did we go from being emperors with the Egyptians
to being slaves"
I said
"That's something we got to ask God on that Judgement Day"
That's when I saw her face her eyes told a story
They were so deep so strong mixed with a bit of agony
No make-up to be seen I felt that natural beauty

Wanted to hold her in my arms with no delay
Instead I said
"My names Daniel, what's yours by the way"
She stared at me and smiled "My name Daniel, is Grace"

"So what are you into besides the obvious, our history?"
She replied "Anything real, poems, I'm into spirituality
Peace within myself, before I can spread it geographically
And I don't hit the club with my breast out,
I'd rather be taken seriously"

Had to ask her for her number I didn't want to separate
She said "I'm tired of guys and the games they play
Hope you're different because, I'd love to settle down one day"

Calm certain and humble a definition of a woman
When I thought it, you said it, no need for conversation
Reminding me of Mother in certain situations

We would pray and then lay combined
I'd love you but in reality you're hard to find
My ideal lady Grace still
All in my mind

Believe

Behind the Lines: A Line or Two
TOC

Drugs can play a huge part in physical and mental deterioration. What was once a bright spark can transition into an empty vessel emphatically. A cluster of unknowing participants contributed here.

I saw drugs obliterate the glow of potential in friends from my school days up until now. One experience was working for four years as a door supervisor at a Gentlemen's Club. There I brushed shoulders with the most loyal wives/girlfriends, the most precise business orientated women, the fickle first timers, the kindest of hearts, the disloyal and more relevantly, the alcoholics and the drug addicts. Over the years their beauty and elegance departed like planes on the runway.

Believe

A Line or Two

What happened here miss? It was sky's the limit for you until
You started poppin those pills now you can't even keep still
Sad as every time I see you something is missing
First that sparkle in your eye
Now your teeth colour, it's changing

I see things different looking into the box
When the drug's not in your blood? Your happiness stops
A shame for you the feeling; it's only temporary
Be poor for more
Unfamiliar with or scared to face reality

I'm one of few who see you and I feel it for
Others take advantage knowing you're desperate for that score
So they'll use and abuse then send you on your way
I tried talking but my words you didn't appreciate
What can I do? Besides observe from a distance
Re-collecting memories of when we were infants
Told me about your plans to be business lady
Now it's just getting a hit
Daily

Bitter feelings towards your family
You they deserted; telling me it was unjust
They gave up
The drug reliant you was hard to trust
Wish I could take you under my wing
Elevate you off this land
All's needed is a breath from God
Food, Drink, Understand?

Can't help but think I'm going to continue to see you fall
Until a day comes, I don't see you at all
She Keeps saying:
"It's life's pressures that got me feeling blue that's why I do what I
do"
But your life got worse with what started as a line or two

Believe

Behind the Lines: Alter Ego
TOC

Beyond satisfied with the alterations I had made I was more than aware the 'old me' lived on. He was still in here, content listening to the other (bad) side, the side that doesn't have my best interests at heart. Our ego's chief adviser, an energy that would take immense pride contributing to my downfall.

Believe

Alter Ego

Often we make scapegoat of the obstacles life can bring
In my case and most of ours the real battle lies within
Comments of negativity
False claims
Lack of ambition
The daily life of he
Set up home in my dome
He's the old me
Mad as he use to be my priest
Now he's just paper thin
Shame, even paper has the ability to break through thick skin
Hounded me through life
Feel I can't get away
Waiting to pounce
Like predator to prey
Its sinister plan to make me the man I was
Back in the day

He tells me "relax"
When I must go further
When I miss that target
Labels me as failure
In reality I know I either must try harder
Or the object of my desire was simply for another

Certain times I can mock you
But shouldn't underestimate
Only a push of a button causes a bomb to detonate
If I surrendered to his ways
I'd lose all morals I've put in place
Then you'd abandon me when denied entry through God's gates

I don't know what the future holds
But know who holds the future created me
Listen to Him then paradise it shall be, surely
Or abide by my ego the arch enemy
Whose goal is to make hell, my destiny

Believe

Behind the Lines: Unfamiliar Encounter
TOC

Early memories I was referred to as ugly and too dark by my young peers. A victim of a racist attack in primary school. Insults in secondary school followed. Understandably my behaviour was often criticised.

My life choices and conduct were the subject of severe scrutiny. Negative attention dominated, to the extent positivity gave me a feeling of unease.

Over the years I had developed an ideology where each insult was like a stone, when thrown I would gather it to build a wall, by the time I reached manhood my wall was indestructible. No insult could penetrate, in fact it often tickled my wall and generated laughter.
When applauds or compliments were dispatched, I would peer over my wall with a foreign expression, instabilities crystal as I scanned my nervous system for an up to code way to react. I speak in past tense but the symptoms remain, albeit to a lesser potency.

Believe

Unfamiliar Encounter

Similar to a bat finding refuge in a cave
Find I'm retreating into my box when receiving praise
But standing tall with a smile when the recipient of hate

Reached that state
Unfamiliar when people adore
Negativity the norm love doesn't recur
In search for words
I stall
As I prepared for impact firm like a wall
Because the last time I received love I couldn't recall
So I amble in my armour
Baffled when the bullets are not sent
In its absence I'm susceptible to the tyrants

Undoubtedly, I've felt the warmth at times
I close my eyes and revive…
My first fight;
Strangers asking my I.D so they could cheer my name
Or when she said she loved my poem so much
She read it, again and again
O how my life has changed…

Most of the negativity has gone
But still find my shield a valued weapon
I'm in a world where being so nice is being so wrong
Some don't think twice in this life and you'll get walked on

When will all my barriers be withdrawn?
Is what they inquire
When I no longer exist in a physical form and I retire

Believe

Behind the Lines: Boxer's Memoir
TOC

As an amateur and professional boxer whenever I was told the
name of my opponent a realness awoke within me. It notched
up my focus and ignited a firmer attitude and approach to
training.

This next piece was written in 2008 when I was still an amateur
boxer. I recount being given an opponent that had previously
beaten a friend of mine. I had an additional reason to win.

Believe

Believe

Boxer's Memoir

(Based on 20th November 08 Bout 1[st]Round TKO)

They relayed his name…
My face resembling a freeze frame
But everything in my mind had now changed
The adversary now has an identity
So fighting I'll be most definitely…

I see he as a machine seeking destruction
So I train myself hard until I'm better than him
Punishing my temple – Sorry but I've got to be the best
First steps doing more than what the coaches request
More than just a fight more than a title to claim
Oblivious to the lights snubbing the money and the fame
In search for money, to make, a change
The key to these chains could lie at the base of my fist
Or underneath, my pen, lid…

Similar to the love for my Mother I offer all that I posses
Looking like I just won the wet t-shirt contest
Striking the pad – A thunder storm indoors
First you see the flash then you hear it
The lightning burst
Face creased I grit my teeth
That's just the furnace inside bringing out my beast
The gym now useless as an empty safe to a thief
Replete, I'm beyond my peak
A bear returning to a cave, I retreat
To the echoes of my thoughts and my heart beat…

This game? Near impossible to rehearse
Still revising my four-hit combination bursts
What will be my stance or first punch
Though this could all change in an instant
Confess to some paper or press play on the sound
Limiting my feet's contact with the ground…
Fight Night has come, it's now…

They say boxers possess immense braveness or stupidity
Nevertheless, only a fool denies it's my destiny

Believe

Saw him at the weigh-in conversation he tried to derive
I couldn't respond because soon I'll be trying to hurt this guy

Daniel Mendes representing Queensberry Police A.B.C
Let the show begin
All eyes fixed on the ring with two warriors in...
Standing solo though everyone's behind me
Whether physical, mental or spiritually...
At the sound of the bell I come forth with force
Anxious he's going to hurt me so I hurt him first
If you stay there my friend it will only get worse
I say 'my friend' as I do this with love not hate
Seeking success stumbled upon you in my way
So superior boxing skills I had to demonstrate

Teleporting left and right I am hard to locate
He experiences my presence when it's sowed in his face
Threw the dummy he took the bait
Then I caught him with a left cross; it devastates
Pretends he's OK
The umpire's having none
First round TKO
I've won
The ref raises my arm in victory
Then I look up to the sky to Who Made It Be

Believe

Behind the Lines: Concrete to the Sky
TOC

A narrative of a low moment, the characteristics, the causes and the prescription. The opening lines notified my mind whilst walking to work. One of my favourite similes are found in the poem.

Believe

Concrete to the Sky

Deflecting wind off my cheek
Watching the alternation of feet
Searching corners of my mind
Trying to find inner peace
Don't be fooled by my presence
Size or frame
I'm that gentle giant passing by
With feelings to drain
A disaster could be occurring
I'm right at the scene
But I'm walking straight through
Obliviously

My Company I can't escape
These thoughts won't halt
They just rotate
Like I've disturbed a beehive
Finding things hard to shake...
Why I'm so familiar with lies I struggle to believe?
Why I didn't know my friend was my enemy?
Does the woman of my dreams even exist?
And am I the cause of my own illness?
Is my future a sight of illumination?
In need of a message from God's kingdom...

Awaiting peace I retreat
Becoming my own doctor
With this treatment on offer:

> "Seek The Creator Of All Power and advice from Mother
> Then it's only a matter of time until you recover
> The Lord is your shade in the summer, coat in the winter
> You'll hear but don't consider that deceitful whisper
> And soon my child you will prosper"

Whether it takes seconds days or weeks
I know in my heart I've got the best remedy
Exiting quarantine
Raise my head from the concrete to the sky
Thank you for my rescue
The Most High

Believe

Behind the Lines: Grandma & Co
TOC

Every family have their ups and downs, mine is no different with
some of the rifts likely to be taken to the grave. I'm guilty of
cutting ties with certain friends that affected my sanity but when it
comes to family, those ties are imperishable. I'm not the type of
friend or family member that always maintains daily, weekly,
monthly, in some cases yearly contact but each family member
has a place in my heart, if my life was taken for theirs, I would
pass away a proud man.

Believe

Believe

Grandma & Co

This to my strength and my weakness
That is my family
Much love to you
My strength because you make life so much easier to go through
My weakness as for my blood there's nothing I wouldn't do

We may not talk on the phone daily
Or see me every day
Truth is from my heart you'll never separate
Don't know all your favourite colours
Your entire lifeline
But I know the blood that flows in you is the same as mine
At times we'll disagree be insensitive to what the other may feel
Realise all we got is us
The wounds must heal

Whether I've known you from day
Or you're the cousin I met last week
I'd still sacrifice my life for you to keep that heart beat
As for you there's no mission I won't complete

Whenever I step in the ring
Each and every time
Only two thoughts occupy my mind
I pray to God...
Because I'm nothing without him by my side
Then hope after I'm a step closer to taking my family off the grind
Training 6 days a week, so will you see me often?
The answer is no
But note
I do this
For Grandma and Co

This to my Strength and my weakness
Much love to you all
May God bless you and catch you when you fall

Believe

Behind the Lines: A Sister
TOC

My Mother converted to Islam when I was 8 years old. My Mother found an inexpressible amount of peace and contentment within Islam, I witnessed that. Away from the military and unforgiving stereotype that can haunt Muslims there are people like my Mum; warm, loving, understanding, forgiving, demonstrating so much compassion I have often referred to her as a saint.

Undoubtedly a glow and true happiness can be found on the many righteous paths present on Earth 'But I saw what Islam did for my Mother'.

Believe

Believe

A Sister

To the nature of women I love and admire
You inspire
My Muslim Sister…
Beautiful women achieve a spark but Sisters flow with a glow
A look at my Mother; it will sure show
Though material girls think they got it they're gold plated it's true
Only a shell of any value

A Sister in a Hijab will symbolize the purity in this life
With a beauty and strength from The Most High
Gliding with elegance tranquil but strong
To avoid them feeling uncomfortable
My looks I won't prolong
Just a sight of the eyes behind them radiance lies
There the soul is satisfied
As the Lord they will always remember
I have seen it regular within my Mother

Pace the same path always looking to find
Approval from The Most Merciful, Most Kind
When my vision was blurred
Your compassion often provided sight
Blessed is a man with you by his side

Trust a Sister will sin but never falls from grace
She's seeking forgiveness from The Most Great
For serving The Preserver a strong Sister knows no barrier
Another factor inside my Mother

Whether a glistening jewel to a Son or Daughter
The loyal companion to a privileged Brother
Friend or family member…
Your love elevates like a hot air balloon
A route removing my mood from the gloom

This to my Sisters who I rank so highly
Especially the one who raised, me
Sure, any righteous path you will alter for the better
But I saw what Islam did
For my Mother

Believe

Behind the Lines: Dealt with Death
TOC

At this point in my life death was something that had never affected me directly. The first two stanzas are based on the true events that took place in one of my longest standing friend's life. She was unfortunate enough to have lost both parents, both parents who I had met in my teenage years and in adulthood. That was the closest I had come to death.

Following that, I was in London visiting my close friend Simeon Harrison. I recall exactly where I was when he made a comment regarding death. We were standing at a set of traffic lights near Marylebone Station. He said the words, "We are at an age now where our people start to go." I froze momentarily and soaked it in.

My Grandad had suffered with prostate cancer for 10 years, something I wasn't made aware of until the cancer had gained a monopoly on his body. With my other Grandad residing in Jamaica, Grandad Ricky was my closest source to a Grandfather figure.

Before I would even arrive at my Grandmother's I would often hear him singing along to some reggae music, where he was likely to be wearing his white string vest either in the front garden or through the kitchen window which was situated on the ground floor facing the front yard.

Before I began competing in boxing my Grandad and I would smoke together in the kitchen sampling each other's weed. He was never short of advice and a huge support for all of us.
When I began boxing as an amateur my Grandad saw my fights via DVD recordings. He named me 'Dan The Lion' in patois it sounded more like 'Dandelion', this would later be the name stitched on the leg of all my professional boxing shorts to pay homage.

My first funeral I observed a mixture of emotions. The necessary tears, joyous smiles of family congregating and reminiscing. I also bore witness to arguments, physical alterations, a knife being brandished. The magnitude of the scuffle forced traffic to come to a stand still.

Believe

Believe

Dealt with Death

Dealt with death before but not someone too close
My girl's Mom's suicide
Then her Dad was ill
She lost both
Couldn't console her
What I thought I couldn't have spoke…
If that was me Lord knows I couldn't have coped

Couldn't put my arms around you tell you 'it's going to be ok'
Couldn't be there for you day by day
You clung to the bottle I watched you
Deteriorate
"Is this what your parents would want?" - Was all I could say

I remember speaking to my boy, in the capital L.O
He said "D we're at that age now, where our people start to
go" I said "I know" Feeling a presence of worry
A year later those words became my reality

Black suit black shirt black tie and still I'm not feeling smart
Black blood running through my black heart
Means we are destined for that struggle right from the start

Clouds leaking eyes watering
There's arguing; what a disgrace
Imagined my Granddad somewhere this don't take place Stood
in silence hope you didn't see the envy in my face
But would you rather be in this world or at God's gates?

If I said I cried I would have lied my eyes were dry
Now does that make me cold compared to the next guy?
When someone dies there still with us just not in the physical
Life is eternal in a world that's spiritual
I will feel a sadness when I go to my Nan's
And I don't see you there
However, I feel a slight relief when I look at the world today
And you are not even here
In memory of Alvin Smith R.I.P.
My Grandfather
I'll surely see you again, come the hereafter

Believe

The New Chronicles
(TNC)

Believe

**Behind the lines: T.E.A.R.S
(Tragic Events Amass Relentless Stress)
TNC**

Crying as an adult I thought would only occur when someone close to me died. I was wrong. Films, disputes and reflections on my life have dampened my face. Learning a friend had cancer, break ups, my predictions of the future have resulted in the same outcome.

I do conceal the lowness within at times but this poem shows my willingness to admit when those restraints have surrendered and I have embraced the often therapeutic process of crying.

Believe

T.E.A.R.S (Tragic Events Amass Relentless Stress)

Resembling rain descending drains in winter
Mine like a damp wall with an internal manoeuvre
Sensation of a slave ankles bound together
Frustration of life not getting better

Fastening your hood in the storm and still getting wet
The feeling of hope-less-ness
In this test do I undress and curse the skies
Or bow my head 'til out the grey
Sun arrives

Our minds select 'strive or surrender' in stages of stress
When all efforts seem effort-less
Kind words unavailing like a woman's caress
For it's I who holds the key to my happiness

A medicine from the morn I was born
Regularity reduced thus arrives in purest form
An instant reaction or brewed like a storm
To my disposition the ducts conform...
Cases of severity tend to manifest
Hands shaped as my head, the drops transgress...
Some smear thoughtlessly...
Are we ashamed? Signs wane but origins of emotion remain
Discharged or dragged through the dust?
Regardless the occurrence is evermore a part of us:

- A seminar for the future, behaviour change
- Or that tale brought up, again and again
- A deposit for the closet to never proclaim
- Or the portholes to the soul depicting so much pain

I keep secrete not one to declare
He alone knows I am in a state of repair
So hands symmetric, consult The Great
With his will I elevate...

Among the weight on my shoulder and organ in my chest
Again seeking figures of blissfulness

Believe

Behind the Lines: The Dark
TNC

While living in Stoke-on-Trent the EDL (English Defence League) a far right islamophobic organisation with racist tendencies were demonstrating a lot around the city and gathering media attention. I was a competing amateur boxer and worked full time as a door supervisor (bouncer) so in a small city I was relatively known.

One day, whilst watching the regional news on TV I saw a couple of familiar faces marching with the EDL. Most notably, a man whose son I trained with regularly so I would frequently see him at the gym, a man who often attended boxing shows I fought on and would congratulate me upon my victory.

He was interviewed by a news correspondent whilst at the march and for the world to see he looked directly at the camera and belted passionately, "There's no black in the Union Jack". It made me question my circle of friends, their integrity and true feelings towards me. Living in a city where I had no family not only did I feel alone but also unwanted.

Believe

123

Believe

The Dark

If I should die before I wake…
They would cut me up and throw my body to waste
Slash my remains with blades
Through my skin it penetrates
Because for me
All they've felt
Is hate
Yet they smile
Into
My face

How do I classify what is a friend or enemy so cold
If all the wolves that surround don sheep's clothes
Feeling trustful often followed by a sense of regret
My thoughts were high for you now they're…
Basement
I exhale as my soul mellows a slight groan
Does a man who builds a road to the heavens have to travel alone?

I've fought taught
Wrote and spoke
Will I battle until I retire?
Maybe relinquish my revolt?
Or my odyssey disrupted by a sudden halt? …

When they send that bullet into my body
It locates my heart
The blood splatters and this life I am no longer a part
Clusters of bystanders deny
Though their eyes did see
My death was surely an improvement to thee
Alike in our satisfactory
At ease, I honoured the treaty

My end
Was penned…
Right from the start

Heading for the light…
Departing the dark

Believe

Behind the Lines: Grateful to God
TNC

I have always believed in God. I feel he has shaped my life; I didn't always have guidance but I searched and asked for it repeatedly, night after night. With consistency I found clarity.

Believe

Grateful to God

Grateful to God
Words could never express
How appreciative I am
Knowing I've been blessed
For every test
How you've moulded me along the way
Trusting you'll be there for me
Beyond my last day
Thank you for the hard times
Stressed depressed or broke
Knowing you won't instil in me more than I can cope
Every hurdle I conquer I simply land much stronger
With increased strength and wisdom for obstacles in future

Grateful to God
For all that you do
Ashamed because my first poem should have been about you
I'll continue
My life story an author could never create
So all my accomplishments it's to you
I'd like to dedicate
As I strive to return to that innocence state
Hope you'll forgive me for my sins and back when I chose to stray
Me and the devil was talking
He easily won the debate
Now back in your corner here is where I'll stay
I'll be the tree you be the wind
Only in your direction I will sway
Submitting my will to thee who made us of clay

Grateful to God
Last but not least
For everyone you sent my way allowed me to meet
And proud to be...
A small component in a force of a family
They have my heart; I love them, more than me
Pray what you've done for myself
You please do for them
To my Saviour from my soul
I love you... Amen

Believe

Behind the Lines: Barack. Abuma?
TNC

I watched on TV as Obama was announced as the 44th President. I was prepared mentally to witness his assassination as he took the stage and was a little shocked that it didn't happen.
Presidents Abraham Lincoln and John Kennedy died of gunshot wounds to the head for going against the grain and initially I concluded that a black president was too controversial to uphold and his end was near too.

After cross examination I realised the shade of his skin determined nothing, all previous assassinated presidents were white. At that point, I also concluded that it was in fact what he did that could result in him being the 5th president to be murdered whilst in office and the fact that he was 'allowed' to win increased my scepticism. I pondered on whether he was a 'true' leader or just the voice of a superior force and assumed that his colour would be to blame if he failed to impress.

I am grateful for President Obama's appointment, he gave young black children hope in terms of achieving the unachievable. For that he will always be remembered.

Believe

Barack. Abuma?

When you won I was surprised
But did not celebrate
Because you're still a politician at the end of the day
Famous for lies
Painting a pretty picture in a war zone
Telling us what you think we want to hear
This you are prone

Feeding the fiction
The truth? Hidden
The last decent one died... Assassination
And he was white so why all the expectations because of your race
It doesn't mean the same deceptions won't take place
I hope you're true
They say:
> "If it's going to be anyone it's going to be you"

To deliver or be the scapegoat black dude

But what is the President?
A mere spokesman for the system?
Or does he really make the decisions?

Believe

Behind the Lines: I Have to
TNC

Ambition is relentless within me. Untamed it lacks submission qualities. I know I want to inspire people on a large scale: to aim high, live and work righteously but there is that realism within me that reminds me that I can't do that, at least not yet.

I sent this poem to a friend who was incarcerated. In his reply he told me that reading this made him cry. I do recognise the sadness present within this poem, yet I still recognise the overarching message of hope.

Believe

I Have to...

You have a lifetime to shine
Why spend a lifetime in the shadows
Demons took the lead
They just followed
Though I am bold I cannot force a better display
But I have to
Find a way

The Devil wants my soul window shops everyday
Opens his wallet but has never got enough pay
I watch it purchase another prey
I can't make everyone keep theirs... I shrug and say
But I have to
Find a way

Eyes closed they won't watch as I demonstrate
I see shambles
To them? It is okay
They practice pause but I preferred they press play
I can't make them see
But I have to
Find a way

The real I've maintained but they favoured my phoney phase
What use to excite me...
Now? Gets a cold gaze
I changed in time but they want what I was back in the day
I can't change minds
But I have to
Find a way

My lyrics? More than close friends
I nurture them for months
Then give birth through my pens
I bring soul food
They send plastic pretends
Knowledge nowadays is never the trend
I can feed them with my lines but in their minds will it stay?
I can't inspire the world...
But I have to
Find a way

Believe

Behind the Lines: Conundrum in Mind
TNC

As a believer in God I accept a responsibility to give thanks and dedicate prayers to The Almighty. I have ambitions and life goals which I ponder and work towards multiple times a day, being a boxer is a way of life as well as a profession.
I am more prone to wake up early to train or get to work than I am to pray to God. Truths like this form a guilt and make we wonder if I have got it all wrong.

Believe

Conundrum in Mind

Equipped with our aims
A purpose in mind
Something we'd like to achieve before we're out of time
It's when I focus on this it's like...
I'm living too much for this life

Neglecting my faith to make my future bright
Missing daily prayers but working all hours of the night
This is me
I cant deny
Living too much for this life

I ponder The Originator
As I measure how to put things right
My feeble frame useless shouldn't I leave it to Your might?
Instead for my fantasy yes I will still fight
It's me
Living too much for this life

To see the struggle cease along with deceit
Witness my loved ones living at ease
But it seems
I'm risking being burned in immense degrees
Should I be focusing on you and not these dreams?...

Though for my mirage to materialise
These body parts I'd sacrifice
Am I lost?
Living too much for this life

Searching success in this life and the hereafter
But fear I'm neglecting the latter
In my defiance to let suffering be the prequel and sequel to this
chapter
However, shouldn't I just be escaping the fire?

Without you Lord I'd be crawling but here I stride
With my soul and a question in the back of my mind
Will I meet the blaze trying to eradicate the strife?
I pray I'm not living too much for this life

Believe

Behind the Lines: Untold Legend
TNC

Every bouncer (door supervisor) who worked on the front door of a specific club for an extensive period of time will create a bond with management, fellow door staff, receptionists etc. Stephanie Hanson was no exception. We shared countless in-depth conversations. As well as my bad habits she was also well aware of my good intentions. Steph and everyone I worked with at the legendary 'ST1' have residence in my heart forever. I spent 4 years working there full time (my longest period at a job then) sharing many laughs and meaningful conversations; Karly Raymond, Micheal Hall, Daniel Austin, Luke Caci included.

On my last shift there, on the cusp of leaving to embark on a professional boxing career in London, unknown to me, all staff had done a collection to help me on my journey. Outside of the family I had never received such warmth and care. I cried.

Whilst completing a routine shift I detailed my life plan to Steph, shared with her what I would like to achieve and how I wanted to help others. She looked at me and said, "Dan, you're a Untold Legend you are" Stephanie gifted me with a title and inspiration to one of my favourite poems.

Believe

Untold Legend

(Inspired by Stephanie Hanson)

They said I was too laid back but dedication I proved it
Steady pace piercing the pacific like a cruise ship
Coming through I see you
To some I was light to the blind
Paved the way still they refused to find
When I retire in that port
End of my time
Know I gave you my heart with every line

When I die an untold legend
Don't mention who I was
But what I was striving to be
Reaching the promised land
Escaping the alley...

Every 10 fake friends I lost
I gained one true
So as I lay breathless they'll only be a few
In that line passing by
Chain of anguish
Praying they could bring me back with one wish
I'll look by don't cry where I'll reside it is pure bliss
We knew one day it would always come to this

When you speak of me please know
Under pressure I stayed straight
Never did fold
My soul I held dear
Never been sold
Through the years did persevere accustomed to the cold
I will die a legend untold

To my kinsfolk
It's hope...
That kept my spirit alive
I would bow my head
Close my eyes...
Pray I didn't stay underground but reached the skies

Believe

I guess in one way or another
I did arrive :)

Let me apologise...
Any who feel I did neglect
To change the world was never second or third
But the initial project
Eyes open or closed these goals I would never forget
So sacrifices I made I had to accept

Looking beyond a sad face or two
In order to reach a few

At best I was like stitches in the flesh
Repairing wounds was my do's then I would disconnect
At worst I would disperse
Glass hits ground
Your plane to pieces I depleted
As you adjusted to having me around
You said "no" I had to go
King Cold I was crowned
A title profound
Received reluctantly
Though 'Moyenda' was what I did... Embody

Like them theatre shows
Bowing out to applause or groans
Think of me as waiting backstage once my curtain is closed
If you ever catch me peeping through the holes
Be sure and bold
It's just that legend untold

*Moyenda – On a journey

Believe

Behind the Lines: Your Sun
TNC

An intentionally confusing poem. The tone and diction was meant to come across as venting but I wanted the identity of 'the offender' to remain unknown.

Whilst competing as an amateur boxer I progressed to the later stages of a regional boxing tournament, The Midlands Final. My opponent, a highly skilled fighter, was known to my family. Hearing of his credentials and researching his accomplishments at that inexperienced stage of my career my nerves were unable to withstand such pressure.

My Father, a former professional boxer, the first to take me to a boxing gym, who took me on my first run, he was beyond instrumental in introducing me to the sport. I did not become a boxer *for* my Dad but I believe I probably became a boxer as a result of him.

I froze during that final. My Dad, not always correct but always honest was highly critical of my performance. I understood that he loved me and didn't want to see me hurt but when he recommended that I quit and consider a semi contact sport it obliterated my heart. The interpretation then was that my number one fan had lost belief in me. I couldn't remedy that.

I retreated and regrouped, continuing my boxing journey unbeknownst to my Dad. My following boxing tournament was The London ABA Novices, again, I reached the Final. Other than two coaches and one of my gym mates Emily, nobody was there for me.
My opponent was 7-0, 7 knockouts. His seventh victim I watched in person, lay horizontal on the canvas before the bell could signal the end of the first round. This was at the previous stage of the tournament.

After a fairly quiet first round I went on to win The ABA London Novices and upon leaving the venue I confessed the weekends activity to my Dad. I expressed it was something I had to do following my dismal performance in my previous tournament and

Believe

apologised for not making him aware of my antics. His exact words were, 'It's ok, you won, do it again'

'Your Son' was written before that competition. Since then my Dad remained an integral figure in my amateur and professional career. The highs and the lessons, accompanying me to the ring at times and present every single time I fought professionally in the UK.

Believe

Photo Credit: Simon Downing at digitalsportsphoto

Believe

Your Sun

Leant on a wall
It collapsed
Off my feet

Standing firm
The ground crumbled beneath

Stepped in it was shallow
But the sign read deep
Reversed my motion
Had to retreat

You swore you was there
But I will swear you was an absentee
The U.N.I.T became... 'Me'

So I will live like the sun
Lord lay the path I will follow
Standing alone
Me and my shadow

Ground I found alters
Prompting my stagger
I'll be your Sun
With God's sanction
I will hover

Lonely stance I'll advance
Midday in July
Contradicting views I am bemused
Why chose to sigh
Stay refrained
Frown upon my escapade
I work, for The One, Who Made

As your Sun duly sets
This heart will fade pulse diminish
I defined blaze...
Never relinquished

Believe

Behind the Lines: Gravestone Talking
TNC

Having read a book from 'The Mercy Oceans' collective, written
by a spiritual teacher of the highest calibre, I discovered that it
depicts our time and foresees cases where individuals will
classify those who have passed away as the fortunate ones
because of the state of the world. This concept resonates with me.

Believe

Believe

Gravestone Talking

Strolling through the crowd
Look at me I'm green
This the last place I should be jealous so it would seem
Stepping with caution
Everyone else stationary
Gravestone talking
Wandering the cemetery

If only I were among you
If I could be in your place
Unable to gaze here with pride
I stare in disgrace… You are at rest
We in torment
How lucky are you
I am struggling
Obsessing on making it through
To have lived in earlier times
Never breathed these hours
Things are rarely sweet here
Just sours

Free from lies sighs despise and deceit
Intentionally walking you to danger after they take the lead
We have demons in the masses
Their clothing is plain
No red uniform or horns out the brain
At bay they remain until in a position to reign

'If only I was young again'
That's what some elders say
Wish they could turn the clock back is this the foolish way?

With you in my position
I in yours…
You would fulfil this life with a passion
I'm queuing by them exit doors
So I can rest recuperate
Watch a disastrous play
I'll have front row seats on the edge of the stage
With the greats I admired from my heart beat days

Believe

Behind the Lines: Empress
TNC

Raised in a predominantly black family. Strong black women were the norm, beginning with my Mother, Grandmothers and Aunts. Spending time in The Gambia and after visiting Jamaica for the second time I was inspired by my surroundings to record this.

Believe

PhotoCredit: Desrene Mendes CEO of Mendes Creativ

Believe

Empress

Skin dark she glows... Empress
Origins of The Mother Land roots I suggest
When combined I stride with pride
There's a S on my chest
When I see you
See righteousness

By my side I'm truly blessed...

Throughout this conquest
Sisters losing respect
By their stance or dress
A rare find my kind of... Princess
Admiration given, no demand or request
To the lady promoting 'natural is best'...

Whether corn row, afro, plaits or dreads
Reveal minimal flesh
African attire no scantiness
Wins my beauty contest
A gem priceless
Accompany me to all events
Where we can jest
Or tackle issues complex

While the glamour girl simply fails to impress
Nubian Queen it is to you my heart directs
Hair wrapped they attract
Beads round their necks
Perplexed how beauty manifests minus special effects

Guiltless to express
Plenty paint is plain art-less
Seeking humbleness
Our roots your presence reflects
And the future?
Much dependant on your prowess
To my highness
Divine? Yes
Empress

Believe

Behind the Lines: Body of Sin
TNC

Not one to shy away from my errors, 'Body of Sin' addresses my transition from sinlessness to sinner and highlights some of my genuine misdeeds.

Believe

Body of Sin

1985
July the 1st
Planted in me
Yet to burst
Source of comfort
Initial face of purity
Seed yet to flourish and nourish this demon...
Ability
I a sight of innocence
Glowing next of kin
Though steadily evolving was the force within
Engineering...
This body of sin

Sowed in
Sinning in my actions
Sin in my thoughts
I was crossed...
Now the revenge plot starts
Damn these feet they caused grief
Laces indented your jaw
Thanked God for my escape but the Devil I was working for

Lord it's deep I even...
Sin in my sleep
Dreamt I could have been straight but decided to cheat
Disregarded the wife
Rumbled the sheet
After I vowed not to creep

Moans of constant drought
Why I sin out the mouth
Whining about
My endless winter...
It is daily rain and minus temperature
The forecast I deliver
Plus a routine encounter of the system's cold shoulder
Woe is me as I grieve
Upside down grin

Believe

Discontent though my hearts still...
Beating

Functional limbs beauties I have seen
The love of my Mother
Many without these still I sigh and whimper

Sinning with my eyes
Why didn't I just look straight
Ignored the whisper exercised better restraint
Then these hands I reprimand for touching you there
You thought 'forever'
I thought 'never'
Predicted your despair
You saw 'The One'
I sought fun in your underwear
She said me or none but I was gone
Wreckage in my rear

My remorse it's clear

Gazing into space knowing you are there
Praying for forgiveness
When I sinned aware
Questioning my purpose
h20 multiplies out the eyes
Asking I'm not judged by my successes but my tries

Believe

Behind the Lines: Tunnel Vision
TNC

Finding focus is a lonely operation. Especially as a professional boxer/committed athlete. When people around you don't share the same desires and priorities you will feel alone regardless of the numbers. This resulted in me finding an absurd amount of contentment in my own company. Recalling a friend who would repeatedly invite me to parties and similar social gatherings. Following my refusal she asked if I would regret not 'living' if I was unsuccessful in reaching my goal.

I'm unshakable in regards to my self-assigned purpose, I'll 'live' when it is completed and if I don't complete the assignment I don't deserve to 'live'.

Believe

Photo Credit alfenphotography

Believe

Tunnel Vision

And so I'm...
Detached
Like a blind man with friends enjoying the...
Scenery
I'm secluded though there's others that accompany me
In favour of seclusion
It's my mirror I'll reflect
I know they have a plan for us I'll die before I accept
The suits won't rule
In my jeans I will direct
Or relentlessly leaving messages until my very last breath
To die a wise gem not another pebble; one of my many conquests
They say if I fail I will rue the time I did invest
Though wishing I started sooner would be my only regret

Lower my gaze and close my eyes
How did it come to this?
The rat race...
Chasing our ideas of pure bliss
Life transforming faces of pure smiles into visions of unhappiness
I flex my arms and clench my fist

"They won't get me"

But until this frown departs those words are empty

The depth of these thoughts
This mind's conundrum of avenues
In my eyes you'll find my story in greater magnitudes
Forgive me if I breeze past in pursuit of my dream tunnel vision
My life counts for nothing until I complete this mission

Believe

Behind the Lines: Your Grandchild too
TNC

One of my last memories of my other late Grandad were myself
and my older brother sat on the floor in a room my Grandad had
rented while he visited Birmingham, United Kingdom. He sat
elevated and spoke to us about topics ranging from the racism he
experienced as a young man in England to criteria to adhere to
when selecting a partner and the type of friends we should and
should not allow in our circle.

The Grandfather figures I was privileged to be a pupil of may
have departed in the flesh but they left some words that will never
die. The supply of new material has sadly diminished, though I
am surrounded by highly suited teachers passing us by and not
uttering a word.

The divide between generations is compelling. How can the youth
mature without the superior guidance that ambles by on a daily
basis? Is this the unexplored antidote for our wayward younger
generation?

Believe

DANIEL "D. SERVANT" MENDES

Believe

Your Grandchild too

Granddad's speeches ceased shortly before the funeral
With synchronised tears
But the echoes remain like he resides in these ears
He would clutch an opportunity to dispense his knowledge
Sat on the floor legs crossed
We'd look up and pay homage
When I see those aged
Especially of Jamaican descent
I remember you and wish like you
They would share some content

If they could talk to me be my sat navigation
Knowing I'm wrong I'm longing for
Validated direction
Sterling teachers too negligent to grant a lesson?
What are the children without the older generation?
Some have poured scorn
Criticised our display
But hide wisdom
Show us the way

I thought I'd initiate
That's why I wrote this to you
Please spare me a minute

Like I am your grandchild too

Believe

Behind the Lines: Soul Sorry
TNC

I advise anyone seeking their truth to do more than vocalise it.
Execute it. Everyone's belief regarding our creation and the
existence of the supernatural will not be identical. I have faith that
God knows that and he is also aware that not everyone will
believe in Him; this is where our deeds come into play.

Along my search I read from The Bible, The Quran and some
spiritual teachers, some content connected with me some didn't. I
returned from my quest believing God is not exclusive to any
particular religion not even to people who believe in him. It is my
belief that God will reward an atheist or agnostic if their good
deeds outweigh the bad. That is MY certainty.

In relation to the title, I accepted our souls were sent to us from
the heavens during a certain stage of our time in the embryo, pure
and unexposed to the harsh realities of life.
This take on our souls made me apologetic to mine (my soul) as
me and him know, my journey has been far from heavenly.

Believe

Soul Sorry

Before my first breath
Before my Mother and Father laid and kissed
My soul did already exist
In the heavens
Duly praising his name
Yet to be united with me and this 'free will' brain

Of all the greats you could have graced
The Creator chose you when he blew
Introduced to a life of less light
More blue

So I send apologies to my soul
Sent from pure bliss
Would you have hesitated in your arrival if you predicted this?

Innocence to corrupted brains
Pure springs to toxic rain
Devotion to idol games

I lower my eyes to sympathise
Demoted from the skies
A mansion
To flats high-rise

From feasts to starvation
The Great One to the slum
Enter me
Temporary incarceration

The ego defies...
Though together WE'LL thrive
If I did not succeed
I tried

Believe

Behind the Lines: Underground Legacy
TNC

I would like to take this opportunity to mention my older brother Anthony Mendes in greater detail. The admiration I have for him due to what he has overcome, to be who and what he is today. Fights, suspension from school, arrests and poverty - rarely does success emerge.

My brother made a life changing and incredibly brave decision to join the army. Following the tragedy of 9/11 deployment to Iraq for UK soldiers was rife.

I recall being on my way into college, sitting on the upper deck of the 98 bus on Oxford Street when I received his call. He informed me that he too would be stepping into the warzone of Western Asia. Once the call ended, I cried instantly mulling over the worst outcome possible.

Thank God my Brother made it home from Iraq following 5 months of being stationed there. I will never be able to comprehend how he got through that. One minute would have been unendurable for me, the fear would have rendered me hysterical or frozen in a coma like state due to the reality of the environment.

My brother completed a four-and-a-half-year term with the British Army including a tour in Ireland, but his days of being a hero were definitely not behind him.

Upon his departure Anthony found it very difficult to find work. I was residing in Stoke-on-Trent working two security jobs provided by two different agencies, one during the day and one during the night, I would come home from one job, shower, change clothes then go to the next job. Often going days without sleep. I found humour in the situation and would jokingly speak out loud to my bed longingly during my change overs, saying:

"Listen, I'm sorry, I know I have been neglecting you lately, but on Tuesday, me and you are going to spend some quality time together"

Believe

An example of our brashness and how we always look out for each other. I suggested my brother stay with me in Stoke where I would 'give' him my daytime security job. My brother would take my SIA badge (License to do security work), complete the shifts, I would calculate the hours once I was paid and give him his wage. Thank God there was never an incident where his identity came into question.

Succeeding these times, Anthony applied to join the Fire Service perusing employment at various fire service locations, including Wales. Until finally finding home in our home city of Birmingham, where he joined the West Midlands Fire Service in 2009.

His courage and resilience know no boundaries and if our story is never told again after this is read it doesn't take away its legendary status. Our underground legacy.

Believe

159

Believe

Underground Legacy

"I wish I was older" said a young Daniel Mendes
Now I'm sitting here grown and finished
With a CV of grave mistakes triumph and tragedies
Battles scars and weights, you can't convert to kg's

But my resilience I flaunt
Maximum effort, effortlessly
Me and my Brother authors of our underground... Legacy
Smiling at past tears
Shedding tears on the past
Tear ducts activating pondering the pain forecast

Grateful for the light loved ones and infinite laughs
The support left me speechless but we spoke through our hearts
Hostilities made me a man of peace
Failures made me unable to surrender
Darkened days eventually made me the illuminator

We often tire of this existence despite our ceaseless strength
Don't just cover ground with those shoes

Represent

Believe

Behind the Lines: The Sponge
TNC

My calm and collected show made me appear emotionless at times. Many felt this entitled them to say or do whatever they pleased with zero filter, assured by my previous behaviour there would be no aftermath. In best part they were correct however sporadically my feelings would revolt and would verbally march over the catalyst, trampling mercilessly until satisfaction was met.

Here the repeat offender would look at me in shock while I, bemused, struggled to conceive their contentment in ambushing me prior.

Believe

Sponge

A Bathroom utensil
Resembles I
Begins with 'S'
Something we use to wipe
Me and the sponge are similar in type

Rain showers
The pain programmed to absorb
External factors weakening my force
Still I come forth
Progressively useless I continue...
I have reached my limit!
Watch what you do

Full with the weight and strain it is true
The slightest stimulus I will rain on you
Give me a drop I will surely leave you drenched
Held masses of pain, hear the consequence
Previously you flooded me with issues did not repent
I was the vacuum in all events

Reached my capacity
Previous behaviour cannot conclude
The one-way traffic you gave returns in multitude
Pressure imposed now descends upon you
Out of blue
You never expected it to

A sponge reaches its peak then must discharge
I do my best to contain
Then comes the Avalanche

Believe

Behind the Lines: Memory Lane
TNC

Memory Lane depicts a time of existence I cherished dearly; I feel a degree of honour to be able to say I witnessed the pre social media era. I was alive when great men and women (some mentioned on the first stanza) walked the same planet as me.

A highlight of my life was getting to shake hands with Nelson Mandela when he visited my Junior School in 1993. My school, named after the great man, chose me to meet and greet him upon his arrival. I consider Nelson Mandela and Muhammad Ali to be the last two great men we had on earth. It is overwhelming to know I shook hands and locked eyes with one of them.

Back then celebrity culture had not become so fickle or hypnotic. People of depth had a portion of the limelight. Good deeds seemed so much more authentic. I deem that as the rug unrolled, it became less genuine.

Believe

October 1993 ⑤News

Believe

Memory Lane

I countersign a time
Where great women and men were followed by millions
Minus the blue tick
Ali, Mandela, Teresa
Jewels I shared the earth with
The blind are followed by many
Many given sight by the blind
I witnessed the extinction of the revolutionary kind

People doing good deeds for fame and praise
When I was younger minus the camera
My poor Mother still gave

Where gaining friends only meant face to face
Fists merging handshakes or an embrace
Now we're scrutinising profiles fake

When raps had depth and only the genuine survived
To those knowledgeable having access denied

President Lincoln and Kennedy's fatalities
Died for what they believed
To those who prefer everyone else to die
For their greed

Is it me?
I see no inspiration on the screen it's lame
My heroes now reside on

Memory lane

Believe

Behind the Lines: Caged Comrade
TNC

I have been asked a few times about who this poem was about, was it my Mum or partner? On each occasion they have been wrong. This poem is about my relationship with myself.

Believe

Caged Comrade

When I came into this world I should have known from then
Only you would be closer than any family or friend
Looking for acceptance
It was staring in my face
Developed as I did
Like a simultaneous race
Often treated as if I do not even care
Yet when abused you stayed right there
Neglected with a glare a little worse for wear

Queries like infinity routinely continue
I'm seeking your advice with all that I do
Regardless of how major or minute
You keep me going like exhale through a flute

Still other's well-being over yours I often choose
The thought of aiding another I struggle to refuse
Reassured as you would do the same too
Our custom: kindness taken as weakness may come true
But for me and you that's nothing new

I gave my heart to others that was never a issue
Yet the day they betrayed
You changed your view
Because you wanted the best for me
As I wanted for you

The times my morals fade
Temptation nearly causes a crack
You keep me in line
Like them trains on a track
Still when I misbehave I have you to blame
Either standing by or participating
When I act lame
My head hung
As you too look at the floor
Promising me you won't do it no more
We voyage through life combined we stride
Praying any hurdles are soon rectified
Our union? A force when we unify
An alliance of reliance between I and I

167

Believe

Behind the Lines: Muddy Grass
TNC

My history with women is highly concentrated with guilt and regret. The times I have been hurt by the ladies in my life do not mirror the amount of times I have hurt them. Verbal or physical assaults I am innocent of. My guilt lies in my nonchalant attitude and dismissive nature which is often that fatal blow. Whether it's my immaturities or priorities either can lead the way and I follow robotically. I may not show the guilt and regret but it is often felt.

Believe

Muddy Grass

Temptresses gems confusions
My encounters with women
The gems all escaped
Temptresses came running
With my eyes on the prize I didn't appreciate
What personality was worth they were gone within days

The gems came then they went
Though I am seeing one through
Those previous came at a time I was too immature to
She told me she loved me
I brushed it away
Or when that one proposed I laughed in her face

Many solely long to be longed for like so
I felt nothing
I was stone cold
With devastation in your eye I stepped to the side
But at times not to feel is the only way to survive

Some I bugged until we hugged then stayed snug
During the period we call 'honeymoon'
Portrayed herself perfect though it logic faults seep through
But this was as if in you were two people
So my relations rarely conclude
As you changed
Hey maybe I did too
I can't leave me
So I leave you

Resembling that of a demon child
I have seen oceans come out their eyes
And I strive to make the heart demolisher
A figure of my distant past
I caused enough teardrops to make muddy grass

Believe

Behind the Lines: Therapy
TNC

I may not credit myself on many things. Contrary to 'Muddy
Grass' I do acknowledge that I have brought elation and clarity
to many of my friends and family, this poem focussed on my
female friends and my sensitivity affixing effortlessly. A trait I
feel was cultivated by my Mother.

Believe

Therapy

When tears leave your eyes like occasions in winter
Call on me
I'll be
Your shoulder
Unlike leaves on trees
I will remain
Bonded by hearts
Feeling...Your pain

Reciting words that register as a soulful melody
If you are cold
I will bring
The heat
Rescue from the arctic
My arms complete your attire
Unlocking every pore where frustrations harbour

Call on me
I'll be your tissue
No need to wipe or smear
Just be near
And Queen the stream will
Disappear

Internal masseuse
My instinct soothes
Surpassing surface penetrating roots
It concludes
Windows no longer drowned
Profound how Mother got me... Programmed

Releasing my embrace
Weight on your shoulder emigrates
The gaze...The smile shapes
Tell me it's I you appreciate
Unaware you have also caused me to elucidate

The sparkle I now see
Gave me one within
A purpose A reason for me...
Living

Believe

Behind the Lines: FAULTering
TNC

Physically focused. Even when I deviated mentally. My training or work would never suffer. On the surface, I represent an always efficient, disciplined trained athlete but on the inside, I resemble a weak, confused slave to temptation. Akin to insecurities and faults.

Believe

FAULTering

Concern is the theme:
Am I getting more wayward with every heartbeat?
Like the morals that built my road is crumbling beneath me
My walk tells no lies
My heroic actions deserve a theme tune
But my thoughts and frequent trips
Show I have been contaminated by the fumes
Could I sprint through the fire to reach my targets?
Or part way end up a carcass?
Could I be left with just enough flesh to hold my withered arm up
in victory?
Or will the flames destroy what's left of my destiny?

My only sense of security is a gaze to the sky
The Most Low
Seeking The Most High
I want to give the blue a feeling of glee
Those who dream small
A sense of royalty
I can do that just let most of my actions do the talking
Because if you could see my mind, you'd know
I'm 'FAULTering'

Believe

Behind the Lines: Un-friend Me
TNC

An instruction based on the repeated outcome of a host of friendships. I had grown tired of the cycle. Adjacent to this time a friend cut ties with me after I failed to attend her Birthday party. The first of two friends to sever all forms of dialogue for the exact same reason.

Believe

Un-friend Me

Seems it's safer to be my enemy
Than my friend
Disappointing those close
Is my trend
If your heart is in the distance
Throwing daggers
Know you are safer than my friends standing in
Blue showers

Saying

"We don't see you often, what we aren't...
Worth the hours?"

"You were my rock now you're just my
Faulty towers"

My enemies don't want to see me so my absence
Never matters
But for my friends it upsets, even...
Angers
Until they take a step back raising... daggers

Believe

Behind the Lines: Poem COVID-19
TNC

COVID-19 affected everyone in the world. Whether you were that teenager looking over his or her shoulder, wary of police attention during lockdown, or if you were that bachelor or bachelorette staying in isolation missing those sentimental moments with loved ones and family.

The virus created a divide; various theories emerged. I purposely did not address any - I simply stated the facts that I was aware of. When I wrote the first draft of this only thirteen thousand people had died worldwide - with that figure now over eight hundred thousand, the scale of this pandemic is much more apparent.

Lockdown gave me an amount of time I was unaccustomed to having but allowed me to focus on areas that had previously been neglected. Large portions of this book were completed during lockdown.

RIP and condolences for everyone we lost and those who lost someone. A moment of gratitude for those that survived.

Believe

JANIE CRISTINA SALSKOV

Believe

Poem COVID-19

Started December 2019 in China
Killed one then two, over 800 thousand before it was over
Could it have been nipped in the China? Did it have to escalate?
Negligence brought a consequence no imagination would create
It killed in every continent bar Antarctica it escaped
Shook the world more so than any earthquake
They played it down then reality struck
It was the end of March by the time China's death toll stopped
going up
For the rest of the world Corona wasn't ready to subside
Symptoms:
Shortness of breath, temperature and coughs that were dry
They shouted: social distance, isolation, to prevent and recover
And whispered smoking increases your risk for the deadly corona

The government went from a distant relative to our reliance
We'd listen daily subject to our compliance
Known for their lies we hung on every word
They sold toilet roll for £10: it got absurd
People were arrested for leaving their home
The most vulnerable at times the least compassion was shown
Prior Corona people plotted the theft of money
Jewellery of gold or diamond stature
In the UK we had 3 arrested for the theft of hand wash and toilet
paper
We self isolated, prisoners in our own home
It was Mother's Day I just communicated over the phone
The virus exposed the selfish and supersized paranoia
A cough was like the waving of a needle from a homeless heroine
abuser

If I woke up and it was all a dream it would have all made sense
I was in disbelief daily at the reality of events
Competitive sports banned restaurants closed pubs and clubs
NHS were heroes, delivery drivers and some shops even gave
away grub
I did laps around my flat in my dressing gown beard past first
stage

Believe

They said they would rely on teacher assessments to determine
GCSE grades

I watched things on TV rarely got excited
I hoped for them numbers to start going down
So I could vision our freedom from confinement
We need to stay together in staying by our self
See you on the other side
Wishing everyone
Good health

Believe

Behind the Lines: Devil's Food
TNC

Despite the frequent praise I receive now, I am concurrently
notified of my blameworthy past. It obstructs me from approving
this positive recognition. A moment of adoration is
reconstructed into an emphasis of my prior errors.

Believe

Devil's Food

I have caused mass catastrophe
Call me 9/11 or World War One
In arctic mode I have caused nothing but
Devastation
Consuming quantities of guilt
Until it makes me numb
Like I have accidently run over two...
Children
Mirror dusty I stare into space for my...
Reflection
Re-tracing steps trying to figure where my heart has gone
I left no bread crumb
I thought it would be returned in bubble wrap
But it has gone
Taken
Hijack

Watching tears journey down cheeks
Tick the box
I am a sinner
Stubborn in the wrong
I am Osama or Hitler
This torpid organism gazes through your...
Drowning eyes
My heartless body denies the ability to...
Sympathise
Chuckle when told I am sweet
I guess Devil's food I must be
A tempting sight but a merciless
Calorie
I tread alone aware my presence leads to...
Health complications
My absence is not worthy of complaints but...

Celebrations

Believe

Behind the Lines: They Live
TNC

I am an avid fan of horror and science fiction movies. My supernatural experiences consequently fed my engrossment in the horror genre further.
I accept many find the spiritual world far too ridiculous to validate. Using examples of real-life people became my motive for bridging the gap between the two worlds.

Titled over a year after being written 'They Live' intentionally draws reference to the 1988 Sci-fi/horror where the late Roddy Piper (RIP) discovers sunglasses that enable him to see the world the way it truly is.

Believe

Photo Credit: AzadYasin

Believe

They Live

Vision evolving, I uncover things you pass obviously
I squint analysing surroundings with scrutiny
Select a sideways glance or widen eyes at my discoveries
Burdened sight I observe in real life
Impossibilities

Ever seen a lifeless body walk like it just rose from the cemetery
Slurping out a brown paper bag
In the A.M they roam free
Swaying with a stagger no consistency
They crave a drug not blood
I see zombies

A Father killed his Son
Man murders his Mum
Babies raped
Deaths of innocent children
They embrace the darkness abscond from the sun
Leaders craft the demise of an entire nation
Minus red costumes and horns out the cranium
The dominant don suits
I see demons

Tried to put knives in his back
They just bent
Suffering like breathing so...
Frequent
Idly snatches good deeds to out-weigh endless repents
And pain? Only modifies his De-fence
Remains unfazed regardless of the brunt
Infinite obstacles his life is like a stunt
Discredit his sanity
Slander his difference
In my mirror and amongst us are...
Mutants

Believe

Behind the Lines: Clockwork
TNC

Another troubled time motivated me to seek 'Pen Therapy'. I cannot pinpoint the exact stimuli here due to my memory but evidently I was going through a familiar process. One that was becoming like clockwork.

Believe

Clockwork

They say 'hold your head high'
But why? We are all living in shame
How can I look to the sky?
I'll focus on the drain
For my actions it is not pride I am trying to proclaim
I must sigh as I just falter
Again and again

Hand imprint on my cheek
I demonstrate a cold stare
Eyes open but it is clear I am not looking nowhere
You may approach after much hesitation
I am a statue
The brain is in motion

Like a vintage clock, cogs turn for the second hand to tick
All my internal is active
You will only witness the blink
After a whole rotation my minute hand is a sigh
By the hour the little hand moving signals I understand why...

Complete contentment will everlastingly be
The unreachable location
Until my soul is an affiliate of club satisfaction
I apply though my CV is not one of pure bliss
Unable to describe myself as an optimist
My life consists of many days like this
Where only the air I breathe is not negative

Believe

Behind the Lines: Friendless
TNC

Accepting I may not be the most popular person amongst my associates I embraced the ideology of being friendless. Some friends were proud and willing to accept boxing had become my priority, others felt offended that the urge to reach my goals was superior than the desire to spend time with them - This poem was also an attempt to justify my unwillingness to change that.

I disclose a time I dislocated my knee during another London Final amateur boxing competition, this time of the 'Elite' category. Unrelated to the theme I must jovially share an exchange I had with fellow boxer Daniel Evans who I saw in transit at London Liverpool Street Station while I was on crutches, he looked at me saddened and said "You were a good boxer as well" I responded laughing "I'm STILL a boxer, what are you talking about"

Believe

Believe

Friendless

Gave them every last warning
Admitted I was bad news
So stubborn in my views
Before my focus it must be noted
I boasted friends in multitude
Now I hold few
Friendless I maybe
But if it reads 'a great friend' on my gravestone
It means I failed miserably

'Inspired millions, a world changer,
walked through flames to achieve'

Sounds a more interesting read

So friendless I maybe
I grin acceptingly
The time I didn't have for you
Became your grudge against me
The luxury of leisure I limited with intent
To make reality of the dreams that I dreamt
Now you can tell me my cold heart makes me a bad breed
Or understand my sacrifice with my desire to succeed
The red dribble
Bones failing
Remember the crutches I did need
The sleepless nights
The wars
I risk my life
Please believe
For nothing I could feel in the ring
A KO or even if I died
Would hurt as much as if I never tried
So I walk through fearless
Trembling inside
Knowing my actions were justified

Believe

Behind the Lines: Deposit
TNC

Poetry is just that - a deposit for me. I encountered many misunderstandings and misconceptions during my expedition (especially when boxing began its reign on my schedule) this was my counterclaim, my defence.

Believe

Deposit

Confessions and admissions poetry is my depository
Know that with my book of rhymes
I am handing you my life story
Labelled self centred
Stranger
Strange in my ways
My heart resembling the arctic; this all common phrase

Their critique bounced of the surface like a hail storm
I'd stare for a minute then continue the norm
God, I don't request that those I love understand me today
Though I ask the picture becomes HD when eventually I lay

If I waved aside your sober storm
That character was drawn by my fixation on 'The Disaster'...
This life
The remedy
I had to be The Doctor
You wasn't in critical condition so my mental didn't deviate
Signalling your thoughts with that stark wet face
You portraying the colour of the sky or the liquid in veins
I would step past the flame to deal with the blaze

Daily I prayed for change
"Dear God" I asked ya
Then you blessed my working limbs and said
"Go conquer"

Believe

Behind the Lines: My Block
TNC

I have my moments where I lose hope but to date, I always
regain it. The sense of having nothing is one that has trended
throughout my life but many have done great things from the
humblest of beginnings.

Believe

My Block

Anything that elevated was down low before it rose
So one should welcome these...
Tragic episodes
A nod to the stars
Re-focus on my toes
Without struggle there is no progress...
I suppose
Dream of peace tranquillity
My children playing in meadows
But I see grief
Destruction
Warm hearts that froze
I stand tall
Though my shoulders bare heavy loads
Inspire the masses; the mission I chose

So I may say nothing but
Think a lot
Plenty pain but Minimal tear drop
They wanted the same I evolved non-stop
I'll build my empire....
Starting with this one block

Believe

Behind the Lines: The Front
TNC

'The Front' addresses that lie we have all told. Saying things are fine when in actuality they are far from that. I reveal my brief transfixes with suicide and the surplus amounts of guilt that haunt me.

The 'poison' I refer to is the ability to sin. We can't beat it, it will remain until the end.
Concluding I state: if you are not struggling mentally you are blind; I say this because my thought is that only someone who is not aware of the type of world we are living in (or numb to their environment) can maintain perfect sanity throughout his/her existence.

Believe

Photo Credit alfenphotography

Believe

The Front

Occasionally I'm beckoned by an oncoming train
Like it's a way out
Sometimes the glance turns into a stare
Then I swiftly snap out

Incurably opposing this poison
Until my wake
Sins gained momentum since my Summer 85
Birth date

Now I lie daily I act and feel no way but...
Am I meant to say "no" when asked "are you ok?"
Give you The Chronicles of Daniel Mendes
And his current state?

So a tranquil damage proof dude
I Impersonate
Instead of leading you into thoughts
You would struggle to articulate

If you are not cuckoo you're blind
And I've lost every screw
Homage to those in detriment
That never withdrew

Believe

Behind the Lines: Lucky Escape
TNC

I mentioned this may be the saddest poem I ever wrote.
Depression had monopolized where again I felt my absence
bettered my presence. My infinite good intentions did nothing to
warrant my worthiness. I was not suicidal here but I was unruffled
by my death.

Believe

Lucky Escape

To pour a bag of sugar
In to the sea
Or to save a life then they die moments later
Naturally
Preparing a 'goodbye' speech but you are too late
They have already gone
The pointlessness of my...
Good intention

As I rose this pen I was like a singer with no 'sing'
Or an orchestra with no one
Composing
I closed my eyes and it gave me
Perfect vision...
Suffer on every horizon
Did a 3 60 and saw pain down every avenue
So I did not move
Straight statue

If I could skip this clay shell
Set my heart free
I would be floating in a direction that was heavenly
Looking at my melanin skin and muscular frame
Like it is my ball and chain

Now does this grown man cry
I'd be lying if I said "never"
This possibly the most dispirited combination of words I selected
Ever

Why when I dreamt I was falling to my death I didn't even cry
I sang:
           "Forgive me for my sins and know that I tried"

When I tell you that I am fine
Forgive me for lying to your face
My death no tragedy but a lucky escape

Believe

Behind the Lines: The Sacriprice

TNC

Disgruntled I had to address the catalyst. This poem remained untitled for a period of time until I digested what exactly I was grappling with.
The sacrifices I made for boxing. They all came at a cost. My family, my sanity, the 'Sacriprice'

Most of the occasions I missed on my endeavours are easily dismissed, others I document here were not dismissed in the slightest, I live with them every day.

I came to the realisation that as much as I toyed with the idea of death and suicide, deep within I knew I didn't want to go yet. Not while the mission was in process, yet if I were to fail outright, diminishing my purpose, my urge to live would become feeble. Hence my association of failure with death.

Believe

200

Believe

The Sacriprice

Radar mute as I pass shoes
No one qualifies to march in mine
DON'T EVER SAY 'YOU UNDERSTAND'
BECAUSE I KNOW YOU BE LYING!
This vertical face, low pulse rate; the truth it denies
The worry and the fears this ambition derives
When I look you in the eyes and tell you without a blink
'I'd rather die than fail'
That's just my natural instinct
Completing the marathon to get rejected at the line
Dedicating my life to an impossible find?

Missed moments with my Granddads'
They died without a single faculty
Missed my Grandma's birthday when she turned 70
I brush feelings
Including my own
My mind functioning as a 'emotion free zone'
My heart hasn't warmed since that ice eclipsed
You didn't see me cry
The sweat dripped
I call success Freddy as it consumes my dreams
And failure is similar to death it seems

What does a hero do if he can't save lives?
My Dictionary defines a 9-5 as suicide

Labelled crazy so much that now I believe
That these trials chipped away at my sanity

I manoeuvre solemn it may appear that my heart has been frozen
But when I tell you to 'be careful'
They're the sincerest words I have ever spoken
The irony of my contradiction
An ambassador of peace engineered precisely
For demolition...

Believe

Behind the Lines: Tissue
TNC

A vent was obligatory as resentment was reaching exasperation. Only a meagre amount of people know the various layers that merge to complete you. Though many will stake claim and dictate like they have gained a mastery on your elements.

Similar to the pattern of behaviour mentioned in 'The Sponge' I absorb a lot of the criticism, attacks on my character and choice of lifestyle day by day but regrettably I have boundaries, once these are crossed by frequency or severity of action or comment no guilt appears from me by the visible upset my 'cold' response brings, in fact only an empathy towards myself is clear.

My other puzzle was the realisation that my circle of support mainly constituted of new unfamiliar faces, hurling accolades at my small but significant triumphs with limited accountability of my history. While some of those that could actually vouch for my early strives and later gains evaded acknowledgement of my strides.

Believe

Tissue

Unless by you I was raised
You don't know who I be
I incarcerate my rage for the sake of your
Tranquillity
And If you never witnessed my shadows?
You are foreign to a large part of me
When my heart abandons ship leaving a cavity

Sympathy on standby
Mr Freeze concludes
Too many actions without a reaction
I nurse my bruise

Common ground with a...
Schizophrenic
I hear them voices
I just rarely obeyed it
Been too hurt for words
But I only appeared when it faded

I wonder why I get love from the most unexpected places
Only known me for a term but respecting my stages
To those who knew my scars read my bars

Yet still I was shaded

Believe

Behind the Lines: CandyMen
TNC

Originally posted on my social media May 23rd 2020. Two days before the murder of George Floyd. Exactly one month after Breonna Taylor, a lady killed by police storming the wrong address, looking for a suspect who was already in police custody.

The title of this poem was inspired by fictional character Daniel Robitaille. A kind-hearted man who was brutally killed at the hands of racists leading him to return in spirit, cold and vengeful, under the name 'Candyman'.

> *'They don't say good night*
> *They just shut eyes and*
> *Stay*
> *Laid on the concrete floor'*

I am referring of the unsettling conditions of our homeless around the world.

Police brutality is approached. I do not condone the killing of anyone in any profession but when our supposed 'heroes'(the police) our 'go to' for help have formulated a reputation for killing and mistreating individuals from a particular ethnicity a response is imminent. Not all police officers are bad but these occurrences are too often for them to be all good.

The hypocrisy amidst the authorities and the elite is disputed. Leaders can call for war knowing innocent children and civilians will die. When police unjustifiably kill, justice can only be hoped for and *IF* justice is delivered it is celebrated emphatically when it should be normality.

Our government approves and benefits from the sale of alcohol, cigarettes and cannabis smoking paraphernalia while two of the leading causes of death are heart disease and cancer - with smoking the leading cause for Coronary Heart Disease. Somehow putting a sticker and a graphic image of the direst effects of smoking make trading of this slow slayer kosher.

Believe

Believe

CandyMen

Why did integrity depart?
Will the system acquire a heart?
I was small and had big dreams
Now I'm big my dreams are small
Displeased
Although I'd love world peace
My focus is getting through the week
I used to want it all
But now?
Just to fund what I need

They don't say good night
They just shut eyes and
Stay
Laid on the concrete floor
We let go of dreams
So we don't catch poor
Can't stop grinding when
They keep taking more
Products are shrinking but the prices
soar Sure

And...

Dear ethnic minorities
Yes
They place people in power with
Racist tendencies
So peace and equality
Become mere fantasy
Like a mouse in a house dodging traps
Envious of the freedom of cats

Now listen before you criticise
I read Officer killed on duty
I couldn't sympathise
When police brutality is world wide
Lady killed on suspicion of being
someone
Who was ALREADY inside

Believe

I watch the news and conclude with my own views
I don't fear immigrants or hoodies and the youths
The coldest of all you see in suits suits

You see, they are not against murder
They just want to be the only killers
And I have figured they are not against drugs
They just want to be the only dealers
And no, you can't have those weapons
But they are pulling triggers, triggers

I wasn't born thinking negative
My heart once occupied much bliss
Then they executed their plan
And it's hardened my spirit like Candyman
Candyman

Believe

Behind the Lines: Resilience
TNC

I had taken a loss in the ring, it devastates. My first loss as a professional boxer was in Macedonia. On my way back I was sat on the plane thinking:

'If this plane crashed right now, I would not care'.

 Funnily I reversed those thoughts immediately when the plane experienced minor turbulence.
Regardless, apologies for the tone of those initial thoughts but that is a case of the gloom morphing my rationality. Coinciding with my mental state when I wrote this, following my second professional loss.

Believe

Resilience

Anyone taken a loss
The ring or in life
Darkness became your pillow
Sanity briefly sacrificed?

The shadows and I allied
Thoughts coal
Ink like
But defeatism? I never identified...

Even optimists insist cloudless days scarcely manifest
Though imperishable is a beam to the left of our chest

Believe

Behind the Lines: Pep Talk
TNC

My preference for pep talk is that it is not sugar-coated, the negative thoughts that pester me are addressed too. My grievance with the world, the stumbling blocks we encounter, the resentful friends and hard-hearted ambition get a mention.

The term 'turning a blind eye' was partly used here. Some things we choose not to see or ignore. I'm simply stating even the side of me that doesn't want to take notice; the world is in such disorder even my 'blind eye' can't dismiss the crisis.

Believe

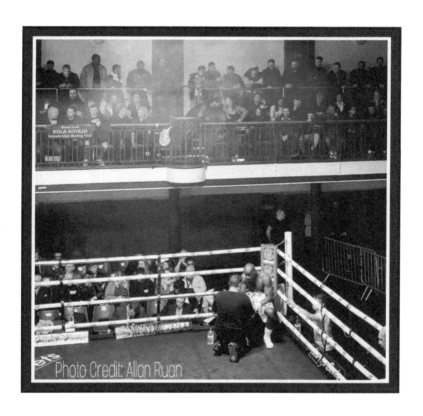

211

Pep Talk

I see outside
My blind eye can't deny it's absurd
But you have got to love living
More than you hate the world

In the rain don't complain
Just adapt
Can't surrender to the times
Because we're stronger than that

When they grumble that you've changed
Feel a sympathy it's true
Tragically years later
They are still the same dude

Loved ones will see you scarcely
Visits? Never in a bundle
Your ambition is wild
Why? Because we're living in jungle

Believe

Behind the Lines: Until I Phantom
TNC

Fatherhood. indeed miraculous. It supersized my urge to live a productive life, one that could be gained from, one that they could be proud of. 'Until I Phantom' was written for my current and any future children. It is my pledge that I will be there for them until I die.

Names of Royalty: King, Royale, Prince, Royal all appealed to me. Firstly, my belief that we should all view each other as royalty. There is no superior race, creed or bloodline as we have been made to believe. My second reason was built around my intent to make them proud of who and what they are.
As a child, I was made to feel subordinate because of my colour, to the extent that I wished I was not black. I want them to know their worth and be reminded of it constantly. Their name will also serve as a message from their parents that they will declare everywhere they tread, never forgetting what their mother and I think and believe about their existence.

Fatherhood brought me a new threat, an advanced terrifying vulnerability where if my child experiences any discomfort, emotionally or physically, I can feel it too, sometimes at an even greater magnitude. My emotions and frame of mind are no longer my property, they gained access to that the day they were born.

Believe

Until I Phantom

I thought I was ready to die until I watched you live
Earth's endurance of evil had me focused only on negative
Until 'The Fridge' with God's grace Fathered his opposite
The Shadow met the glow
A Demon found heart for his Saint
I've beckoned my last day
Now I want untold time to better acquaint
Take pride in your name but know we all are Royalty
Sharing embraces on your birthdays and worst days
Until I phantom effortlessly

I went from being idol to trying to build a legacy
Pulled by many they all required a piece of me
But in you I found my tranquillity
And another reason to be grateful to God eternally
Trust in Him even your blink has His sanction
I'll provide for you with His will
Until I phantom

Aside family ration your energy please...
Those that demand the most should receive the least
Let charity be unforced or it'll wobble your inner peace
Don't fall victim to guilt trips, silent treatment or tantrums
Your Father's love flows in abundance
Until he phantoms

The thought of you harmed breeds an internal tear
Your beauty? It's origins remain unclear
You are meant to be half of me
But how does lead produce pure gold
I shouldn't be hard on myself so I'm told
My love for you brings fear, an infringement, futile to fathom
- Its birth accompanied your birth and it breathes
Until I Phantom

*The Fridge - I acquired many nicknames on my journey, some
sparked a feeling of disrespect, some escaped undetected, some
made me giggle. When I was called 'a fridge'
for my lack of emotion it made me laugh, the creativity was
impressive.*

Believe

Photo Credit: Simon Downing at digitalsportsphoto

Appreciated more than you will ever know

Mendes

Believe

Lightning Source UK Ltd.
Milton Keynes UK
UKHW020632130921
390483UK00006B/55